# From Cosmos to Canaan

*The Bible in Verse*

— JOCK STEIN —

Sacristy
Press

**Sacristy Press**
PO Box 612, Durham, DH1 9HT

www.sacristy.co.uk

First published in 2018 by Sacristy Press, Durham

Sacristy Limited, registered in England & Wales, number 7565667

**British Library Cataloguing-in-Publication Data**
A catalogue record for the book is available from the British Library

ISBN 978-1-910519-96-7

# Preface

To begin with, this was just a poem on every book of the Bible, which I shared with a number of friends. I started writing them because I love the Bible, and because I found a vocation to write poetry once I reached the age of 70.

But who exactly is going to read such a book of poems? Many poetry readers are suspicious of the Bible, and most readers of the Bible aren't into poetry. And bookshops may not know how to classify it—is it theology or poetry?

It is both, of course. All my life I have enjoyed crossing boundaries and gently tearing up labels. When you focus on what people are for, rather than on what they are against, you often come together. And even when you meet someone with whom you disagree, you can learn from them.

That goes for books too. C. S. Lewis wrote an Introduction to a book by the early Christian theologian Athanasius, called *On the Incarnation*.[1] In it, he said we should always be reading books written in different ages. We will see their shortcomings, no doubt—but they will probably be immune to the errors of our time which we don't notice.

For many people, the Bible is "just an old book"—without any modern science and bound by the culture of its times. Perhaps it is just such a book which can shed light on our own times and our own lives. I have certainly found that to be true; it begins a dialogue with the issues of our new century, and in a strange way it also remains relevant to our modern personal concerns.

John Robinson was a pilgrim setting out for the new world of the Americas on board the *Mayflower*. He said he was persuaded that "the

---

[1] Athanasius, *On the Incarnation*, St Vladimir's Seminary Press, new ed., 2007.

Lord hath more truth yet to break forth out of his holy Word". Many books have been written seeking just such truth, but no book (to my knowledge) has ever used poetry in the way I have attempted to do.

The whole Bible in poetry and prose would be far too long—so to be manageable this volume is about the first six books, known as the Hexateuch. To make the book more accessible I have also introduced a friend, giving her the name Jean Sharpin. While she knows less about the Bible than I do, she knows considerably more about poetry, though she doesn't write poems herself.

A word about the poems. All good writing is more than "information"; it seeks to draw the reader or hearer into the story—but the poems I have written are of many kinds. Some are "teaching poems" which do have a good deal of information, whereas other poems are "exploring poems" which pick up on a single aspect, or one character. If some poems don't speak to you, leave them for the moment, and enjoy those which do.

The poems are also in many styles, as the writing of the Bible itself has many styles, and while I have tried to choose a style which fits a particular passage or a particular book, there may be no immediate correspondence. Some of the poems are simple, and rhyme (and so might be called "verse"), while others are more complex.

T. S. Eliot used to say of a good poem that, even if you don't understand it all, you want to read it again. That's certainly true of the Bible, and I hope it may be true of this book.

# Acknowledgements

My thanks to the original four people who read my poems and encouraged me to write a book: Irene Howat, Emma Hunter Dunn, John Miller and my daughter, Dorothy Ogilvy. Irene also kindly checked my Scots language.

Iain Provan generously read the manuscript and gave me the benefit of his wisdom as an Old Testament scholar, and David Fergusson graciously encouraged me with the project.

Many more people—poets, teachers, theologians and folk with an interest in the arts—read bits of the book and made helpful comments, among them Claire Askew, Paul Burgess, John Cross, Roger Garfitt, Alan Hamilton and members of his congregation, Sam Hosain Lamarti, Angus Morrison, Jonny Pott, Catherine Simpson, Lance Stone, Luke Walton. I also thank Tyne and Esk Writers (of which I am currently convener) for their encouragement. All these people are not, of course, responsible for any remaining faults, nor indeed for any of the views expressed.

Bible references if not directly to the Hebrew (or the Greek) are from the New Revised Standard Version Bible, copyright © 1989 National Council of the Churches of Christ in the United States of America. Used by permission. All rights reserved worldwide.

I am grateful to my wife Margaret for her constant support, and the way she puts up with a workaholic supposed to be in recovery mode.

# Contents

# Genesis Part 1

*Genesis* means "beginning": the beginning of the universe, life, humankind; the beginning of the children of Abraham; the beginning of the Old Testament and now the beginning of this book. The Bible is full of poetry and story, theology and history. The way in which they blend and balance is the stuff of scholarship. What they mean and how they matter is a challenge to every age and to every one of us.

That includes Jean Sharpin, who will become an important contributor to this book, in her own way, though her use of the term "challenging" was a bit different—a kindly word she used for a book which did not quite hack it in the modern world. When I suggested that the Bible was a book which had changed the course of history, her eyebrows lifted just slightly. "Poetry used to do that," she said, "Now it's science."

"Theology was once known as 'the queen of the sciences'," I pointed out.

"That was then," Jean said, "We live now."

Jean and I share a love of poetry. We both came to it late, I following a career which centred on the ministry of directing a conference centre, Jean after teaching science (and some philosophy) in an Edinburgh school.

I said I was going to write poems on every book of the Bible. "OK," Jean said, with her eyebrows firmly in place. "Send them to me, and I'll read them." So I did. But I told her she'd need to read some of the book of Genesis for starters which, I'm glad to say, she agreed to do.

**In the Beginning (Genesis 1:1—2:3)**

Seven days to make up everything
from cosmic dust to humankind.
Six days of speaking, one of resting,
days of seeing all was good
in origin, in process and potential.

Seven days to write a poem, sing
a symphony to keep in mind,
hint of word and spirit dancing,
birling stars and swirling galaxies,
making purpose out of chance.

Who knows what other worlds
may sense of their Creator?
We have this book,
we have ourselves,
we have a new beginning.

# Making it up

"I like the idea of God 'making up' things," was Jean's first comment. "I always thought the Bible was a great work of imagination."

"Imagination is a great word," I said, "and we call poets *makars*. The trouble is, 'poetry' is now used for something that is imagination and nothing more. Jews and Christians and Muslims believe that everything started in the eternal mind of God. But we can see and touch creation, which suggests rather powerful imagination."

"Hmm. I suppose it depends how you make the connection. The poet William Merwin wrote about light flying through the world, unconcerned about whether it actually arrived. Just like Stevenson's 'to travel hopefully is better than to arrive'. All that is just poetry, and you don't need a Creator to enjoy it."

"You don't," I replied. "But my take on that is God's generosity. God gives us the freedom to enjoy everything God has made, whether or not we know God's there."

"Do you realise you repeated 'God' about four times in that sentence?"

"Yes. God is more than just a person, and God is certainly not male or female. That's our bag. But I admit, at my age, it's hard to get out of the habit of using 'he' and 'him' for God."

"Well, I won't mind if you slip up," said Jean. She is nearly as old as me, after all. "But back to business. I used to set sixth-formers the old question, 'Why is there something rather than nothing?'"

"What did they say?"

"Some said God, some waffled, and one bright kid said that the universe could make itself."

## Nothing Much (Genesis 1)

Nothing is banal—how typical of nothing
that it contradicts itself immediately –
whatever nothing is. But take that contradiction
back behind beginning, *creatio ex nihilo*:
what clustering possibilities, leaps in
understanding, may lead science and theology
to bed, for ever yoked as yang and yin,

"Well," said Jean, "At least you don't agree with Stephen Hawking when he said that philosophy is dead."[1]

"No," I said. "And I suppose, after Ayer tried to reduce philosophy to language games,[2] this is the latest attempt to close it down."

"But you don't say 'science and philosophy' in that poem. You say 'science and theology'."

"I could easily have written 'science and philosophy'. There are different angles on what is true, different kinds of wisdom."

# So what is true, anyhow?

## Questions, Questions

Just who are you
to claim what's true?
And who can say,
"Yes, come what may
I'll walk my talk
my whole life through?"

We humans must
keep questioning
(a trait that shapes
superior apes),
and what we ask
is everything.

Well, why am I
around at all?
And why is there
a world so fair
to meet our need
(but not our greed)?

To query "How?"
is technocratic:
to query "Why?"
is quite emphatic
that we're more
than meets the eye.

But over "What?"
and "How?" and "Why?"
the question "Who?"
is what I cry:
not, "What is hot?"
but "Who am I?"

"So how does Genesis answer the big 'Who am I?'" Jean fired at me. I said I would email her if she made sure she got to the end of chapter 3.

Genesis begins with two creation stories: chapter 1 covers the creation of everything in the universe before human beings, and chapters 2 and 3 are about one man and one woman in a garden and what happened there. Chapter 1 is concerned with animals rather than humans; in chapters 2 and 3 animals are secondary to humans—an obvious sign that we are dealing with theology[3] rather than history in the modern sense. Each story uses a different name for God, which is the first hint that the Old Testament has different strands, put together later by Jewish scholars in

Babylon (the place of their exile in the seventh century BCE). This is what makes the Bible so much richer than a book by one person could be.

"The book of Genesis simply assumes that God exists," I said to Jean. "These early stories help us know things that science cannot teach us. Why are we here? Is there anyone to thank for this marvellous world? What is the place of humankind? Is there a basis for marriage? Are there limits to how we should exploit nature?"

"Big questions. I found I had to work things out as I went along—most people do, I think."

"Yes, I have a friend who knew Latin, and he said it was *solvitur ambulando*—we work it out on the journey."

The Bible shows us a way to think and act, and the testimony of Jews and Christians is that this way makes great sense and blesses human life. We prove the truth of the Bible in experience, not in some intellectual way—but we can think about it, and we can talk about it.

I quoted the poet William Meredith to Jean when we were sitting below Edinburgh's National Gallery having coffee. He said we need to see things from different angles, appreciate the contrasts. The sheer variety of God's creation requires this.

> In the beginning, God made the world:
> made it and mothered it
> shaped it and fathered it,
> filled it with seed and the signs of fertility;
> filled it with love and its folk with ability.
>
> All that is green, blue, deep and growing,
> God's is the hand that created you.
> All that is tender, firm, fragrant and curious,
> God's is the hand that created you.
> All that crawls, flies, swims, walks or is motionless,
> God's is the hand that created you.
> All that speaks, sings, cries, laughs or keeps silent,
> God's is the hand that created you.
> All that suffers, lacks, limps or longs for an end,
> God's is the hand that created you.[4]

## Science, theology and philosophy

"You said there are different angles on what is true," commented Jean, "but do science and theology belong to the same triangle, as it were?"

"You should read what Jonathan Sacks says in *The Great Partnership*—especially his 'Letter to a Scientific Atheist' near the end."[5]

"Yes, but what do *you* say?"

I drew a breath and tried to explain.

"Both are concerned with what is true, but science examines the world of nature (which includes us); theology seeks to understand God and his purpose (which also includes us). They share a certain humility; scientists develop theories about the universe, but such theories are always liable to be overturned by later discoveries. Likewise, Christian theologians develop doctrines, but don't claim to have God tied down for ever in what they write; they simply seek faithfully, with God's help, to respond to what is revealed in the Bible and to listen to how others have understood that down the ages."

"So theology develops, like science?"

"Sometimes, new evidence affects both disciplines. The observations of geologist James Hutton and naturalist Charles Darwin changed views of the age of the earth and the development of life, which had wide implications for both science and theology. A simple way of distinguishing the two is to say that science tries to make sense of what is in God's world, while theology tries to make sense of what is in God's word. The Bible itself tells us to 'search in the Lord's book of living creatures' and read that."[6]

Jean commented, "Ideally, theologians and philosophers and scientists should be talking to one another. Edinburgh was a great place for that once. You could go out for a walk and bump into all kinds of people we now call famous."

## David Hume

His home swallowed by the makeover
of St Andrew Square, Davy Hume
has taken refuge on a High St plinth,
his wavy hair in green tinged bronze:
great excoriator of religious rot,
bare-chested, as befits a philosopher
determined to pare the apples
of conventional thought down
to the core, and spit the pips
at prejudice.
             Upon his knee
he balances a stony reputation,
labelled by some wag "a good book
has no ending", flagging up
a dialogue still pending with more
than natural theology.

## Can a scientist be a believer?

"Hume was a bit sceptical about trying to suss out God from what we see in nature, wasn't he?" said Jean.

"Yes, and rightly so. In Genesis, God speaks things into being, gives them order, but is not so tied up with them that it would be sacrilege to investigate. Therefore a biologist like Richard Dawkins can look at the world, be overwhelmed with wonder, but still be an atheist."

"Are there any scientists today who are believers?" asked Jean.

"More than you might think. Francis Collins, discoverer of the human genome, is a Christian. Further back, Einstein spoke of James Clerk Maxwell as the greatest scientist since Isaac Newton. Maxwell's favourite hymn began like this:

Lord of all being, throned afar, thy glory
> flames from sun and star,
Centre and soul of every sphere, yet to
> each loving heart, how near."[7]

"But Maxwell was living in an age when everyone was a believer!"

"I would have called Thomas Carlyle, his contemporary from Galloway, a sceptic. But fashion and tradition do have something to do with it—otherwise why would there be so many philosophers in America who are believers, and so few in Britain who are?"

"Touché. But to sing 'thy glory flames from sun and star'?" asked Jean rather sceptically. "That's just back to poetry."

"You don't always have to say it's one or the other. Science as such cannot 'find' God—although many scientists do see God's hand in the wonders of nature. Martin Rees, a former Astronomer Royal, was one of the first to write about how the universe seems to be 'fine-tuned'[8] to support life on this planet at least."

"But some scientists think this so-called 'fine-tuning' is a matter of chance."

"Only because they invent an infinite number of universes. To me that is like the medieval discussion of how many angels can balance on the head of a pin. As it happens, there is a hymn tune called 'Genesis'. It was written for a song which puts fine-tuning the other way round: 'Think of a world without any flowers . . . animals . . . people . . .'"[9]

We are extraordinary people. More than even the higher animals, we are "conscious", we can reflect on the mysteries of life, and the wonder of something as ordinary as a handful of soil. The following week I had a new poem to send to Jean.

## Soil (Genesis 2:7)

A farmer sees crops,
another sees germs;
A miner sees clay,
another sees worms;
but God saw a man
joining earth dust and stardust,
a journey together
with time and with trust
that the soil and the seed
and the rich DNA
would advantage the world
and not crumble away.

"So," Jean said when we met again, "it's about time and trust: God gives time and we give trust, is that it?"

"Trust begins with God. Making anything—a poem let alone a universe—is an act of faith that some good will come out of it for somebody. Genesis 2 is about God making two human beings and trusting them with a garden to look after. That comes just after God declares that everything in the world, including humanity, is good."

"Stardust is popular nowadays. Funny how at funerals going back to stardust is the new take on shining like a star for ever. 'Dust to dust' was more realistic."

"Early poets who knew the Bible used that image, though modern poets are more likely to use images like stardust if they are upbeat, or silence if they are called Mark Strand."[10]

# Human life

We know little about the first hominids.[11] The first two chapters of Genesis give us an ideal picture of human beings, made to be like God. That must mean many things, not least that when people see us, they might be able to see something of God. We are put in charge of the world, and while that gives us a mandate to understand it through science and enjoy its riches, it also means we must preserve it in good order for our grandchildren. That we are failing to do. Notice that humankind was made to be vegetarian (1:29–30)—only later were people allowed to eat meat (9:2–3).

While Genesis 1 and 2 are concerned with "the big picture", they are also about the rhythm of life and the gift of place. They balance the greatness and the frailty of humankind. A Jewish rabbi said that a man should carry two stones in his pocket: on one is inscribed "I am but dust and ashes" and on the other "For my sake the world was created".

Humankind is created "male and female" (1:27)—the image of God requires both women and men. In God's original intention, men do not boss women, kings do not rule subjects, masters do not have slaves. The Hebrew word for husband also means owner (ba'al, which is also the name of a Canaanite god); however, the Bible in 2:25 simply uses "the man" and "his wife".

### Sideways (Genesis 2:22)

Trust God to get the angle right.
Not top-down stuff, so Eve and Adam
prove who has the bigger head.
Not tootsie-footsie, leaving couples
swerving, jinking, playing games.

Go instead for lateral thinking,
keep our gender well on side;
after all, a gentle ribbing
is what men and women need
to keep them human, mute their claims.

"Well, at least there is a bit of equality there," said Jean when I showed her this poem. "I'd like to think I feature in some of your poems."

"We all feature in a good poem about human beings in general—just as we all feature in these Bible passages. That's what makes them relevant."

These chapters were edited by people living in an exile whose conditions mirror much of modern life, and right at the start of the Bible we discover that this book is not just about understanding the universe and the place of human life in the cosmos; it is about what we face each Monday morning. Genesis 1 may describe a week before all weeks, but the wonder of creation and the ambiguity of human life are played out in our lives each day of the week. Genesis 2 may be a story about an ideal garden, but it has featured in countless poems, like Edwin Muir's "One Foot in Eden":

> Yet still from Eden springs the root
> As clean as on the starting day.[12]

"Muir went on to describe what happened when our feet left Eden, didn't he?"

"Indeed—but that is chapter 3."

## Getting it wrong

Genesis 3 tells us the story of "the fall". Adam and Eve together disobey God, going beyond the limits God set in an effort to add to their knowledge. They find out more than they bargained for, and are sent out of the garden. Life begins to decay, to crumble away, after Adam and Eve have eaten the forbidden fruit. They mess up in the garden, and the wider world garden is also messed up. The ground is cursed and barren (3:17–19). The Garden of Eden was a place of work—but now work is sweaty and unrewarding.

I was working on a poem which had a pun between "original singer" and "original sinner", and decided to send it to Jean:

## Sorry is a Difficult Word

John Knox said it, once or twice,
but Queen Elizabeth turned him down.
Alex Salmond might say it yet,
and dine with Trump in London town.

"Eve's fault it was, not mine"
– the first of many lies dreamed up
to foul the ways of church and state
with muck that might have been cleaned up.

"It's in the genes, nae doot o' that."
The old precentor shook his head,
original singer, prophet carrying
double doom: fell down dead.

Of all the blessed "I am" sayings
in the book, this one alone
is left for every John and Alex,
Donald, good Queen Bess to groan.

"Those Highlanders had no knowledge of biology—fancy thinking of a sin gene!" said Jean over a drink in "The Outhouse".

"True—but the idea of original sin simply means that sin is part of our human nature, just as you can speak also of original goodness. People are capable of magnificent goodness and incredible folly, and we all travel somewhere between those two tracks. Often it's 'both/and', not one or the other."

"The mind boggles at some of those characters admitting they were wrong, I agree. I suppose by 'double doom' you mean the link between sin and death, Adam not being allowed to eat from the tree of life?"

"You know the story, Jean. It doesn't seem to end well. Yet there is a change of tone in the text. Adam starts to see Eve as an equal, not just an extension of himself,[13] and God provides clothes for the couple—God is still committed to his creatures. There is some good news at any rate."

# Cain and Abel

"Do you know who has taught me most about the rest of the book of Genesis?" I said to Jean. "Jonathan Sacks, former Chief Rabbi. His book about terrorism, *Not in God's Name*, has got a profound analysis of sibling rivalry, and most of it comes from Genesis. Sibling rivalry is one of the big themes, starting with Cain and Abel.[14] When God accepts Abel's sacrifice, not Cain's, Cain gets so angry that he kills Abel; when God challenges him he tries to excuse himself with the notorious question, 'Am I my brother's keeper?' (4:9) and God tells him that his brother's blood is crying out from the ground. Later, in chapter 9, the connection between blood and life gets spelt out."

"That story has always puzzled me," said Jean, "I mean, why did God accept Abel's sacrifice of lamb and reject Cain's sacrifice of grain?"

"Until you look at the meaning of these Hebrew names, it is not obvious why God accepted grain and rejected lamb, as both are used in sacrifice. The name Cain means 'go-getter', whereas Abel, from his Hebrew name, is content to be just 'a light breath'—but God's breath—and those names teach us that God is not after the quality of the offering but the quality of the one who offers it."

"Thank you," said Jean. "That ties in with Jeffrey Archer's novel, too. Kane is the privileged achiever, and Abel the man of humble origins; and it takes generations before the families are reconciled."[15]

"John Steinbeck took the same story into *East of Eden*. And he uses Genesis 4:7 to show that humans have freedom to choose right or wrong."[16]

Abel is the first victim in the Bible. This led me to reflect on who are the victims, the people of humble origin, in today's society. Who are our Abels, the light breaths who are seldom noticed, and who are our Cains, the ruthless grabbers, the go-getters?

## Abel (Genesis 4:1–10)—Scots version

Wha ur ye, Abel?
Colombian cottar, Feegie Pairk squatter?
Toon drap-oot, tuim flap-oot,
pastit or wastit bi Governm'nt cop oot?

Whar ur ye, Abel?
Hodden doon, trodden doon tae dust again?
Yer bluid is sae lief, it cries oot tae God
and tae a fowk makkit lyk im.

"I wasn't brought up speaking Scots," Jean said.

"Neither was I," I replied, "but I heard it so often I felt it was part of me. I admit I usually send Scots poems to a friend, and she is kind enough to check them for me."

"You'd better translate Feegie Pairk for starters." That was easy enough. "Ferguslie Park."

"How about an English version?"

"OK," I said, "but remember that when you translate a poem into another dialect or language, you normally have to change one or two things to get the same sense across."

## Abel (Genesis 4:1–10)—English version

Who are you, Abel?
Colombian peasant, Fagie Park resident?
Urban drop out, hopeless flop out
pasted or wasted by Government cop-out?

Where are you, Abel?
Hounded and pounded into the dust again?
Your blood is so precious, it cries out to God
and to all the folk made in his image.

"That poem is not very nice if you actually live in that part of Paisley!" said Jean as we were discussing where we were brought up ourselves. "Ferguslie Park has already been labelled 'the most deprived area in Scotland'!"

"Yes," I replied, "but I know some wonderful people who come from there. I can think of a minister with a great heart for young people, an academic with a pawky sense of humour, and the wonderful May Nicholson who founded the Preshal Trust."

"Why do you suppose Genesis tells us we are made 'in God's image'?"

"So that people from poor areas of Paisley can discover they matter as much as well-heeled Edinbuggers!"

Towards the end of chapter 4 we are told what happened to Cain and his descendants. By his seventh generation (and seven represents "fullness" in the Bible) we reach Lamech, so violent that he kills someone just for striking him. The desire for revenge, and the rationale of forgiveness, will appear again and again in the Bible. Whereas God limited revenge by putting his own mark on the murderer Cain, Lamech killed in revenge for a mere injury. Later, a law will be given to limit revenge to "an eye for an eye" (Exodus 21:24).

Chapter 5 then fits in a different birth list, the line through Seth. These genealogies are often used as a pregnant pause in Bible narratives; great story-tellers (like Shakespeare) often give their audiences a break in the flow of the story, for similar reasons. Next, we are told again that God made human beings to be "like himself" or "in his image", but that Noah will be the only one living in that way.

## Noah and "God's word"

Many cultures have stories about a great flood. What is special about chapters 6–9 is that the word "covenant" is introduced. God makes a covenant with Noah, and Noah has to agree to it by doing what God tells him to do. It is not the same as the covenant God makes with Abraham later on, but it has two things in common:

- God takes the initiative, the man has to respond
- God makes a covenant with one for the sake of all.

Jean had been reading on in Genesis. "In poetry you can say God's lonely and show him feeling stuff like us, as in *God's Trombones*,[17] but it's all over the story of Noah too—God enjoys the smell of a sacrifice, God talks to himself, God shuts the door behind Noah!"

"I know. Some think of this as rather primitive, but it does show how God is really involved with the human race, not remote—quite something when you are talking about the Creator of all that is. He really comes down to our level. John Calvin used to say, 'God talks with us simply, like a nurse with a young child.'"

"God *talks with us*? I thought the Bible was a book about olden times."

"The belief that God still talks with us today in the Bible is one reason why the Bible is called 'the word of God'. The Bible is also the word of human writers, which is why we can study it, analyse it, question it and so on."

"Got you, I think," said Jean. "So it's like the universe. You can study the universe as a scientist, you can live in it as a human being, and you say you can study the Bible, and live with it. But calling it God's word is like saying God created the world; it's an act of faith surely?"

"Yes, provided you realise that faith is not blind—while it can't be proved, it is still reasonable, it involves our minds. If we get as far as Deuteronomy, there is a command to love God with all our hearts (which in Hebrew thought includes the mind)."

Like a coin, the Bible has two sides to it, although it is one book. We can make one of two mistakes: we can reduce it only to the word of God, which leads to "fundamentalism", or we can reduce it only to human words, which leads to "liberalism", in which case we choose the bits that seem to fit our culture and our outlook, and dismiss the rest. Unfortunately words like these become labels of abuse—far better to be both "fundamental", in that we keep a basis of respect for Scripture as God's word, and "liberal" in that we interpret it with a freedom of enquiry and concern for God's best intention for the human race. Scientists are familiar with this "both/and" approach—light, in both waves and particles, being the classic example. We meet this often in the Bible, not least when we ask who Jesus Christ is.

It also helps to remember that God teaches us through stories, which are sometimes about things that happened, or memories of what happened, and sometimes are parables. Just as we have two creation stories at the start of Genesis, so there are two flood stories which have been put together here, to make different points (compare 7:2 with 7:8, for example). We need more than one angle on God, otherwise we might pin God down too comfortably.

Two other guidelines when we read the Bible are:

- to understand the context
- to discover if other parts of Scripture give us a different angle.

For example, Noah's sons are told "to have many children" (9:7). The context is the aftermath of a great flood, when the land is empty—but in other contexts people might be wise to limit the size of their families. Again, an old story about Noah leads him to curse the line of his son Ham (9:18–27). People have been known to use this to signal racial inferiority, whereas chapter 10 (let alone the rest of the Bible) refutes this by singling out a descendant of Ham (Nimrod) for praise.

### Noah's Triolet (Genesis 6–9)

The rain comes down for forty nights,
the rainbow puts the world to rights,
that's what the good book always says.
The rain comes down for forty days
– the rainbow's one of many ways
to keep God's promise in our sights.
The rain comes down for forty days,
the rainbow puts the world to rights.

"I've only just discovered the triolet," I told Jean, "it's an old verse form."

"What's it good for?"

"It's a repetitive form. These old forms were useful when stories were being passed on in verse for folk who were not used to reading. Just as the Bible stories were passed down, in days when people knew how to use and develop their memories. Just as people still learn the Qur'an off by heart—I have a friend who did that as a teenager; he said it took him two-and-a-half years. Here I use it to repeat the contrast between flood and rainbow. That is a symbol for the contrast between sin and salvation, evil and good, trouble and rescue, which gives the Bible its pulse and its relevance to the human condition."

## The Tower of Babel

From one angle, this famous story is an early human attempt to explain why people speak so many languages (Babel is like the Hebrew for confusion, and like the English "babble"). But equally it shows the folly of thinking that technology is what matters, rather than language.[18]

"You would say that, of course!" said Jean.

"Well, a contemporary economist did write that ancient poets 'shaped and established reality and truth.'"[19]

The story is presented to show how a false pride in human achievement leads to confusion and failure. It is the last of several "separation stories"—husband from wife (chapter 3), brother from brother (4), sons from father (9) and now people from people. We meet the name Babel, or Babylon, for the first time, and later in the Bible it will become a symbol for wickedness and arrogance. The spirit of Babylon is alive and now well dug into the western world.

In the popular game jenga (*kujenga* in Swahili means "to build") a solid tower of wooden blocks is put on a flat surface, and each player then has to withdraw a block and place it on top; eventually the tower gets so shaky that a careless move brings it down, leaving the last successful player as the winner. But in the Bible story, God judges the builders in an oblique way, so that they stop building before it collapses on them.

### Failure (Genesis 11:3–4)

Saddam Hussein aspired to build a greater Babylon.
He failed. But we failed too. We brought him down
but never built a new life for his people. Chaos reigns,
the bitumen that held those ancient bricks in place
still shapes the foreign policy of western nations,
proves that human greed and arrogance still rule
our politics. Here oil is king, not God, or common weal;
confusion bubbles, nations fall apart and fail.

Jean was moved by this poem or, perhaps, not so much by the poem as by the topic of failure. "I have the feeling that Britain is falling apart," she said to me, referring not so much to the question of Scottish independence but to what she sensed was a lack of moral seriousness in recent governments. "I suppose you think it is connected with our loss of interest in the Bible," she continued.

"I do, but it's not like, say, dropping Shakespeare from the curriculum. The Bible isn't a magic bullet. The real issue is that people don't see God as having anything to do with real life."

"You obviously do!"

"That's because God became part of my life when I was a teenager. Before that I had tried reading the Bible and given it up as boring."

"Another triangle, I suppose," said Jean. "When you write these poems you are trying to link God, the Bible and everyday life."

"Poetry is not a mathematical formula. A poem has a life of its own. But it's true that faith does influence what I write. Who we are is likely to feature one way or another in a poem."

Jean asked how the Bible could speak to nations and cities as well as individuals. That brought us back to Genesis, and to the meaning of Babylon.

Humans will continue, of course, to build cities, and Babylon will be used in the book of Revelation as a symbol for the wickedness of Rome which persecutes Christians and Jews. Yet Babylon will also become a city of refuge for God's people, when Jeremiah gives them the message that God is telling them to build homes, settle down and work for the good of the city (Jeremiah 29:5–7). And this narrative, which begins with a man and a woman in a garden, will end with a holy city, the new Jerusalem (Revelation 21 and 22).

I tried explaining this to Jean, and I did point out that a committed teacher was working for the good not only of individual pupils, but for the good of the communities they would live and work in—Edinburgh and East Lothian, in our case. Then I told her that, after that long introduction, Genesis *was* going to focus on one individual and his family—Abraham.

# Notes

1. As argued by Leonard Mlodinow and Stephen Hawking in *The Grand Design* (Bantam Books, 2010).

2. As in his early book in 1936, *Language, Truth and Logic*, where Ayer propounded his logical positivism in opposition to metaphysics and theology.

3. Theology means literally "god-talk", the study of who God may be and what God is up to.

4. From *The Iona Abbey Worship Book* (Wild Goose Publications, 2005). When used in a service, the text is divided between men and women.

5. Jonathan Sacks, *God, Science and the Search for Meaning* (Schocken Books, 2012).

6. Isaiah 34:16.

7. Oliver Wendell Holmes sr, 1809–1894.

8. Martin Rees, *Just Six Numbers* (Orion Publishing, 1999, 2015), p. 4.

9. Doreen E. Newport (Stainer & Bell, 1969).

10. Mark Strand, *Collected Poems* (Alfred Knopf, 2005).

11. A good book on the Bible and human origins is Tom Wright's *Surprised by Scripture* (SPCK, 2014). Read the first two chapters.

12. Edwin Muir, "One Foot in Eden", *Collected Poems* (Faber & Faber, 1956), p. 227.

13. See Jonathan Sacks' book, *Covenant and Conversation: Genesis* (Maggid, 2009), p. 34 (with permission of Maggid Books, © Rabbi Lord Jonathan Sacks).

14. Jonathan Sacks, *Not in God's Name* (Hodder, 2015).

15. Jeffrey Archer, *Kane and Abel* (Hodder & Stoughton, 1979).

16. Vishal Mangalwadi discusses this and much else in his book on how the Bible created the soul of western civilisation, *The Book that Made your World* (Nelson, 2011).

17. James Weldon Johnson, *God's Trombones* (Penguin Random House, 2008).

18. See Sacks, *Covenant and Conversation*, p. 51.

19. Tomas Sedlacek, *Economics of Good and Evil* (OUP, 2011), p. 94.

# CHAPTER 2

# Genesis Part 2

## Abram the Hebrew[1]

The great journey of the Bible now takes us from Mesopotamia right down to Egypt, and back to what we now call Israel and Palestine; away into exile in Babylon and back again; then from Israel out to the ends of the earth. It begins with God telling Abram (not yet Abraham) to leave his home and go to a promised land. God says five words of blessing, to counter five curses found between Genesis 3 and 9. Good is already destined to overcome evil, and those who will bless Abram are many, compared with one who may curse him (12:3). This man will become the source of blessing for all humankind. Here is where the mission of Israel begins.

I met Jean for a meal. We both have pensions, but we don't spend a lot, so it wasn't an old-fashioned business lunch. Who has the time or stomach for these anyway?

### On for Off (Genesis 12:1)

Abram, patron saint of leavers,
ready for goodbye to routine life,
taken with that healthiest of fevers
sick of settling down, and on for off.

"So Abraham was one of the Travelling People?" Jean made this comment after I had tried to explain how Abram took his wife, his nephew Lot, his servants and his livestock, right along the curving trade route down from Haran heading south; how he ended up at a place called Shechem and lived alongside the Canaanites. (Today it's called Nablus.) There he built an altar, before moving on south into the Negeb, the land which Israel took in the Six-Day War and later returned to Egypt.

"Yes," I said to Jean, "he was a kind of Bedouin sheikh, I suppose. And that command in Genesis 12 to 'leave your land' has the deeper meaning of make a journey 'to yourself' as well as 'for yourself', 'with yourself' and 'by yourself'."[2]

"Do you think God speaks to migrants today?"

"Believers say that God does speak to people, but they don't lay down how God does it. It's true, however, that God seems to speak more openly to people by, say, dreams, in Africa, India and certainly the Middle East than in the West, where we are well locked into materialism."

"But even dreams are a kind of imagination, the brain working while we are asleep."

"That reminds me of the words Shaw put into the mouth of Joan of Arc in his play. The Grand Inquisitor says wearily to the young woman, 'Joan, those voices you hear are just your imagination.' And Joan immediately replies, 'Of course! That's how God speaks to us.'"[3]

A famine then takes Abram down to Egypt (12:10), where he tries to pass off his wife Sarai as his sister, in case Pharaoh kills him in order to take the lovely woman "honourably". His plan backfires, as it deserved to, but he ends up with more animals and a bigger retinue. He goes back north as far as Bethel, and by this time he is so wealthy that he and his nephew Lot are about to fall out over grazing space. Abram, wanting peace, gives Lot the choice of where to go (13:8–9), and Lot chooses to live in the valley at Sodom, leaving Abram to occupy the hill country of the Canaanites.

## Canaanites and conflict

"These Canaanites," Jean said, "I thought they were the enemies of the Israelites?"

"That was much later on. At this stage, they were neighbours whom Abram respected. Thinking of them always as enemies has painted the Middle East in pretty dark colours.

"There was some fighting, though," I continued. "The king of Sodom had a loose alliance with his four neighbours, including the king of Salem, Melchizedek. They were attacked by a stronger alliance of four kings who had been accustomed to rule the whole region; Lot and others got captured and taken north of Damascus. A fugitive came back to report to Abram, which is when he gets called 'the Hebrew' (14:13). Abram and his men went after the raiders, routed them and rescued Lot."

"Not bad for a bunch of shepherds," commented Jean.

"Indeed. But it ended with a rather strange meeting. There is this fellow Melchizedek, king of Salem, who is described as 'priest of God Most High'. We're told he brought out bread and wine and blessed Abram. Abram then gave Melchizedek a tenth of everything he had. Much later, Jewish Christians remembered all this."[4]

"Salem? There is an American town of that name—linked with witchcraft, I think."

"Not from this story. The name means 'peace'—think of the Hebrew *shalom* or the Arabic *salaam*—and it will become the city named Jerusalem, revered (and fought over) by Jews, Christians and Muslims."

## Jerusalem

"Pray for the peace of Jerusalem",[5]
a prayer revived by Teddy Kollek,
genial Arab mayor of Jerusalem.
City of conflict and combustion,
city of international education;
city of stones and ancient bones;
city of wonder, though the thunder
of its past rolls past the present
and makes the future nervous.

"A lot of us are nervous about the future," said Jean. "Did you know I have been diagnosed with Parkinson's?"

"I did wonder a little. When did you first suspect?"

"I've known there was something wrong for a year. In some ways it was a relief to get the diagnosis—I don't like living with uncertainty."

"You may or may not want to read them, but the Irish poet Micheal O'Siadhail wrote a whole book of poems about his wife, during the time she had the same illness. It's called *One Crimson Thread*.[6] I can lend you a copy if you'd like."

"Thanks, I'd like to see them. I'll tell you whether I like them or not. Now, back to Jerusalem. I've always thought it an odd sort of city. It was in the middle of Greek culture for a while, then under Roman rule, but somehow it kept its own identity—even though today the Old City has all these different quarters, and a Temple Mount that's quarrelled over."

Simon Montefiore said that the history of Jerusalem was the history of the world—a gloss on Disraeli, and perhaps others before him. There is a theological angle to that—in the Jewish nation we see our humanity at its best and at its worst. We honour its intellectual and cultural achievements, but when we dislike what we think we see, we persecute its people. In 1977 the Israeli Government invited the Moderator of the Church of Scotland to Israel, and President Ephraim Katzir told Tom Torrance that Scotland was the one country in Europe where Jews had not been persecuted."

"Is there a reason for that?"

"Well, here I am guessing. It might be because we always took the Bible's Old Testament seriously. It might be because we are a small country living with a much bigger neighbour, not always friendly towards us. But if you want a theological reason, maybe we both have a sense that God makes covenant with nations as well as with individuals, though that was stronger for us back in the seventeenth century."

## Covenant and calling

Abram is wealthy, and now has a military reputation. Is he to become a local chief like the king of Sodom? After his meeting with Melchizedek this mysterious king offers him the spoils he has won back for the local alliance. Abram refuses (14:22–23); his God is "the Lord", in Hebrew *j-w-h*, which in Jewish observance is just "the name" and which others pronounce "Yahweh"; while he has certainly acknowledged the high God, El Elyon, chief god of the Canaanites, he knows he has a distinct calling from Yahweh. Abram later did put these names together (24:3), and, of course, the editor or editors (and we readers) know there is only one God, with many names. Genesis will soon use two other names—"the God who sees" (16:13) and "the Almighty" (17:1).

"Is it true that every tribe and culture has some sense of God?" asked Jean.

"Most peoples do have some sense of 'a high God'. I expect there are exceptions—some of the Ancient Greeks were atheists. Atheism is certainly not a modern idea. But generally it's true that people did believe in a supreme deity, yet typically this deity was far off, so in normal circumstances people related to lesser beings, such as spirits or ancestors.

"I was told that once two European climbers fought their way up to the summit of Mount Kenya, and found an African sitting quietly at the top. He said he came up every year to meditate. That story differs from more traditional accounts of Kikuyu religion, where God is acknowledged but left alone—*Ngai ndĩgiagiagwo*, God is not to be pestered."

### Emergency God

> Where else should a high God live
> than on Mount Kenya's peak?
> Kikuyu elders knew his home,
> but yet would only speak
> with him in dire emergency,
> not like every week.
> Listen: God must not be pestered.

"Contemporary religions all show some kind of balance between God as far off and above us, to use spatial language as a metaphor, and God close and within us. With Islam, the latter is more obvious in the Sufi tradition. Theologians have two long words for this—transcendence and immanence."

"Spare me the jargon," muttered Jean. "But tell me, do you get both of these even as early as the book of Genesis?"

"Definitely. For example, in chapter 15, Abram chats to God and questions him, albeit using a respectful name. Yet in the same chapter he has an experience of God which fills him with terror. It leaves us wanting to use contrasting words about God, such as awe and intimacy."

Abraham obviously knew that the surrounding peoples worshipped a high God, yet he and his descendants discovered that this God revealed himself to them in a particular way, which set them apart as a distinct people, with a mission to share this revelation with others.

"Are you sure about that?" asked Jean when I spoke about the mission of Israel. "One thing Jews don't believe in is proselytising."

"You're quite right. Certainly survival seems more important than mission—and especially after the Holocaust one can understand that. Which reminds me—I once asked Alexander Broadie, now a retired Glasgow philosophy professor, to write a booklet on *The Mission of Israel* for the Handsel Press. With some help from Henry Tankel he produced a fine manuscript, but in it he argued strongly that Jews did not have a concept of mission, and that it was only Christians who thought they should have. This puzzled me, as I have always thought of Israel being 'a light for the nations', as Isaiah put it."[7]

Jean, who is more of a lateral thinker than I am, had a thought. "A light has a mission simply by being there. When it is extinguished its mission disappears. So perhaps even the survival of the Jewish people is a kind of mission."

I began to wonder if there were Christians who saw things that way also, and that made me think of Christian minorities fleeing the Middle East maelstrom. So many people, so many different sects, and those in power usually claiming some kind of superiority, typically God-given. Even Abram could have been forgiven for seeing his friendship with God like that.

"At least they have a country to live in," I pointed out.

"Well," said Jean, "I suppose the covenant was always about land."

"Yes, five times in Genesis God tells Abram he will bless him and give him descendants. On three of those occasions, he adds in the promise of the land of Canaan."[8]

## Whose covenant, whose land?

"Is that promise, that covenant, unconditional?"

"A lot of ink has been spilt on that one. In my opinion, the answer is yes and no. 'Yes', in that God's commitment to them does not depend on the Jews being faithful. 'No', in that when they are unfaithful, there are consequences. The obvious one is the way they were taken from the land of Canaan into exile in Babylon. The Old Testament tells us this was because they started to follow some of the worst local customs, like child sacrifice."

I wondered whether the long-running sore dispute over the land of Israel was at root a clash between this covenant made to Abraham and something like the "Palestinian covenant" adopted by the Palestine National Council in 1964,[9] although others see it as simply a dispute between two peoples over land. But I thought we should postpone a discussion on that—there are so many different sides to the issue, and to the meaning of covenant.

At this stage, however, Abram is living in peace with his neighbours—he has given his nephew room to live, and the land is not too full. But he and Sarai have no children. Sarai persuades him to accept her slave-girl Hagar as a second wife—not unusual in that culture—and Ishmael is born. Hagar begins to despise her mistress, who then ill-treats her (16:6). Hagar makes one attempt to run away, and that story will continue later. How easily our attempts at a workable compromise come apart!

### Speed

> How we love a rapid fix
> in families, church and politics,
> with methods often such a mix
> of panic, fear and dirty tricks.

When Ishmael is thirteen, God again appears to Abram and spells out the terms of the covenant. Abram has already believed what God has promised him (15:6), and the practical terms are twofold:

- walk before God, with a blameless life (17:1)
- circumcise your male children (17:10)

The practice of circumcision is not unique to Israel, and there are hygienic reasons for it, and for the timing,[10] but for Abraham and his descendants it was a sign of God's promise. The later *bar mitzvah* and *bat mitzvah* Jewish customs celebrate coming of the teenage years and adherence to the Torah (Jewish teaching)—things that we do, rather than things that God does.

In this context, Abram is given a new name: Abraham, father of nations. Sarai is given the name Sarah. Like the ages in Genesis 5, the ages given to the two may be symbolic—but the meaning of the situation is clear enough. Although previously Abraham has believed God, now he laughs at the idea that a centenarian and a ninety-year-old can produce a child, and hopes that Ishmael might be his heir. God says no, the child of the covenant will come from Sarah, and be called Isaac.

"So Ishmael lost out. I expect the Qur'an has a different spin on that!" commented Jean.

"Strangely, the Qur'an does not mention God's promise to bless Ishmael. It does say that Ishmael and Abraham together built the ka'ba in Mecca, which is a bit odd as Mecca is not mentioned in any other document until the fourth century AD. In another place, Ishmael and Isaac are mentioned as a blessing to Abraham in his old age.[11]

"The Old Testament does give a blessing to Ishmael," I added. "When God chooses some, he does not necessarily reject the others. At an earlier stage Abraham asked if Ishmael could be his heir; the text tells us God heard his request (17:20), and promised Ishmael a blessing, with the prophecy that he would become 'the father of twelve princes'. Josephus[12] thought that the Arabs named their tribes after these twelve sons of Ishmael, but those tribes don't exist any longer."

"People are so mixed up today—while no doubt there are individual Jews, Christians and Muslims who are descended literally from Abraham, no race or religious group can claim that kind of racial purity."

"Indeed not—if you decide to trace your DNA, it always contains a lot of surprises."

## A blessing and a judgement

Three visitors now arrive when Abraham is having a siesta; this is described as "The Lord appeared to Abraham" (18:1). Abraham is surprised, but gets Sarah to prepare a meal. He is even more surprised when they tell him that past-the-age Sarah will have a son. Later in the chapter the three become one, and it is not clear whether it is God or an angel who is talking with Abraham. The story is captured in the Icon of the Trinity by Andrei Rublev, now in a Moscow art gallery.

### The Promise (Genesis 18:1–15)

Three visitors, and eastern hospitality.
Three men, though you can liken
them to angels. Three persons of the Trinity
in later thought, as in the Rublev icon.

Where did they come from? We're not told.
Why did they come? To make a promise
Abraham caught in faith, "You're not too old
to be a father", on the premise

that our God is father of biology
and much beside, yet shares his mind
through conversation, for ontology[13]
is *being* shown to humankind.

Sarah laughed, in wonder or in scorn,
then covered up. God gave a nod
and said, "Your son will still be born,
for nothing is too hard for God."

The three men, who are sometimes three and sometimes just "the Lord",
look at Sodom, and the Lord then warns Abraham that Sodom will be
destroyed for its wickedness.[14] Abraham, aware that his nephew is in the
city, starts to bargain with God. He suggests that if there are fifty righteous
people in the city, it should be spared. The Lord agrees. Abraham knocks
him down to ten, and the conversation ends.

Prayer has many facets, and this dialogue illustrates one of them—
prayer as a conversation in which you remind God of what God is like,
what God has promised, and what the situation seems to demand.
Abraham simply appeals (with great respect) to God's sense of justice,
and the Lord is happy that he does.

But it seems that Lot is the only good person in the city, so it will still
be destroyed. Abraham's prayer is answered to this extent, that the men
(now just two angels) visit Lot and try to get him and his family to leave.

In the end Lot and his two daughters escape, while his wife "looks back" and is caught by the fall-out. Looking back to the past will become a temptation for Abraham's descendants in the wilderness (see the book of Exodus), contrasted with looking forward in faith and hope.

Jean, of course, knew the story of Lot's wife: "A lot of folk get caught by some kind of fall-out, whether it's a fall-out from the world of nature—which I suppose would also cover O'Siadhail's wife and my own situation—or a fall-out in relationships. Do you feel a poem coming on?"

As I am a sucker for commissions, I pretended I did, and got to work. As a mark of respect for Brighe O'Siadhail I made it a kind of sonnet. When Jean and I next met, this is what I had produced:

### Lot's Wife

Remember her with tenderness as well
as fear. It's not an easy thing to leave
your past life, even when an angel grabs
you by the hand. Her daughters have just lost
their two fiancés, and she cannot quell
the thought: just how will each of them conceive
the future of her line? With that, she drags
her feet a little, resolution storm-tossed;
glances back, falls out of step—too late
to dodge this awful chemistry of fate;
the fall-out from her falling out is fell,
dreadful, catastrophic hail from hell.

Did she and Lot fall out the night before,
when Lot near put the girls outside the door?

Jean just nodded. "Chemistry of fate" was a bit close to the bone. I made a mental note to ask her how she was finding *One Crimson Thread*. We left it there and went on with Genesis, leaving Lot and his two girls safe but pretty sorry for themselves.

The editors now include a further story to illustrate the shameful origins of the Ammonite and Moabite peoples (19:30–38). By the time the Old Testament ends, and the prophets have had their say, it will be clear that no single nation has a monopoly of goodness, and certainly not the chosen people of Israel.[15] And the heroine of the book of Ruth is, in fact, a Moabite.

## The birth of Isaac

There is an interlude, when Abraham is living in the south as an alien, and again tries to pass off Sarah as his sister (20:2), to save risking his own skin. This story is notable for the importance of a dream, the integrity of a local king, and a process of discussion through which a potentially nasty situation is resolved. Later they will again have to resolve a dispute over a well, through a covenant, which in this context is simply an agreement between two people. Abimelech is a king in Philistine country, and he recognises that God is with Abraham, although he is exasperated that Abraham has dug the well on the sly (21:26, in spite of Abimelech's open invitation in 20:15). This perspective is worth remembering when later the Israelites and the Philistines are locked in combat.

Finally Sarah conceives, Isaac is born, circumcised and weaned. But then Sarah sees Ishmael playing with Isaac, becomes angry (21:9) and again gets Abraham reluctantly to expel Hagar, along with Ishmael. (You would expect Ishmael to be in his teens by this time, but in the story he is still called a child.) Thankfully, an angel comes to Hagar and promises her a great future for her son. He becomes an archer, marries an Egyptian wife and does not reappear until Abraham dies.

"I've been reading ahead," said Jean, "and I see that Abraham remarried after Sarah died. Why couldn't he have made Hagar his new wife—make up to her for the way she'd been treated?"

"Interesting you should say that. That's exactly what Jewish tradition says happened. Abraham must always have felt he had wronged Hagar. When she was first driven out, she went to live at an oasis or well (be'er) called Lahai-Roi (16:14); it was near there that Isaac was living before he got married (24:62), when Abraham was still alive, and it was there that Isaac settled finally (25:11). The text does say that Hagar made her home at Beer-Lahai-Roi: so it's possible that she had both the young men close to her after Sarah's death, and the tradition says she was renamed Keturah. There is so much behind the Bible text that we'd like to know!"

What we *are* told is that both of Abraham's sons were together at his funeral—and this poem acknowledges the Jewish tradition about Keturah:

### Isaac and Ishmael (Genesis 25:9–11)

They planned the funeral together,
these half brothers, living stronger
separate for half their lives.

But with Abraham dead and buried,
the chosen son moved south,
perhaps to join his other mother

Hagar, at the well of Lahai-Roi,
with God's blessing spilling over
to the stranger life of Ishmael.

God takes a long view. Abraham had two children, Ishmael and Isaac, and, although Ishmael fades out of the story, God also promises him a destiny (21:13); some Muslims trace their ancestry from him, and it has yet to be seen what this will lead to.[16] Here again is a "both/and"—the blessing of one (Isaac) does not mean the cursing of the other (Ishmael). And the choice of one people (Israel) is for the blessing of all.

# Child sacrifice?

The text now follows the life of Isaac, heir to the main promise, and concentrates on the command given to Abraham by God to sacrifice "his only son" (22:2). Jean had never liked that story. "You do realise that here is God telling Abraham to engage in child sacrifice!"

"When the rest of a document makes it clear that something is out of order, we should pay special attention to anything that contradicts that. Of course, some folk immediately assume that the 'odd bit' is a mistake, or a corrupt text, or should just be ignored—but by the same token, a story like this would never have been remembered and recorded unless something like this had happened. The real question is, what does it mean?"

## The Binding of Isaac (Genesis 22:1–14)

No social worker: only a father and a son,
and a named protector, there for good or ill.
Isaac—only a child, feeling the question,
dread dissolving his bones to desert mud,
like drops of dessicated hope, his fear felt
all the way from Gaza through to Glasgow,
Eden's loss which touches Edinburgh today.
Traumatised children: but surely also their fathers
caught up in conflict, living with the slag
that dangerously hides hell's furnace melt.

No voice from heaven: only a father and a son,
and a God to test them to destruction.
Isaac—only a boy, stood in, unasked,
to mirror the questing conscience of us all,
"Why, O God, just tell me, why this ruck,
this maul and mess, this splurge of suffering,
terror, cruelty that chills my gut? Why me?
Why all the lies, the cries, the angry shells
delivering hatred to such helpless places?
Is there no future, no rescue from the muck?"

No easy answer: only a father and a son,

and a protector promising the Lord provides.

Isaac—only a youth, walking, thinking, climbing

deep inside the story of a Nazareth boy

who lived these riddles, worked out how to meet

the evil that one day would fall upon him,

all the boiling slag poured out at Calvary,

another scandal story with a stainless ring,

a ring of steel forged from the love of God,

a future proved in murderous Mordor heat.

"No prizes for guessing where you worked, and what films you like to watch," said Jean.

"I've never forgotten what a steelworks is like at night," I reflected. "Seeing an ingot gleaming red in the dark, watching a furnace pour . . . romantic, and dangerous."

"There is nothing romantic about that Isaac story!"

"No indeed. It certainly raises questions, with Abraham so bent on obeying what God says that he is prepared to kill Isaac. It is a strange journey the two of them make to the mountain, with Isaac carrying wood for the offering, his father carrying the fire and the knife. In response to his son's natural question, Abraham replies, 'God will provide the lamb for a burnt offering.' Is that evasive, or prophetic or both? A substitute is indeed found for the boy (22:13), but without that ending, without the rest of the Bible, it could be a blueprint for extremists."

"I suppose the story does make one thing clear," said Jean. "Human sacrifice (especially child sacrifice) is not to be practised by Yahweh's people—if sacrifice is required, an animal will do. While that's not an issue for us today, it obviously was then."

"The story also celebrates wholehearted love for God and the willingness to give up what is precious when that is what obedience to God requires. That can still be very, very hard to do."

## Abraham's family and God's providence

Abraham charges his chief steward with finding a wife for Isaac from his own people back in the city of his brother Nahor (chapter 24). The steward arrives, prays that he will find the right woman with the right response to his request to have his camels watered, and discovers Rebekah, who turns out to be Isaac's cousin—in the custom of the day, a very suitable bride. Verse 12 literally says, "God, give me a chance encounter", and it is through apparently chance events that God provides. The girl duly returns with Abraham's steward and marries Isaac.

In chapter 26, Isaac also tries to pretend that Rebekah is not his wife, just as Abraham did with Sarah, without even being able to claim the half-truth that she is his sister! While some think this a second or third version of essentially the same story, it does illustrate how easily even chosen men behave badly—or alternatively, how God keeps on using fallible people to work out his long-term purposes. Goldingay suggests that Genesis includes three accounts to show how important it is for men (and women) to reflect on their sexuality and how they handle it.[17]

Jean told me that it didn't reflect well on Abraham or his son. "That's one of the things which makes the Bible special," I said, "Its heroes have flaws. And they don't rely on magic like, say, Ram in the Indian religious epic the *Ramayana*. When Ravana takes Ram's wife Sita into his harem, Ram mobilises an army of monkeys, builds a bridge across the Indian Ocean and brings his wife back in a flying machine!"[18]

"Coming back to Genesis," said Jean, who had begun to follow the text more closely, "You've missed out the start of the fight between Esau and Jacob. Why don't you just follow the order of the text?"

"Probably because I'm not such a good storyteller. In the Middle East, stories often wander about, or go back before they go forward. It's a technique to keep people in suspense. We left-brained westerners need to remember that the Bible was not written just for us."

Back in chapter 25, Isaac and Rebekah have twins, Esau and Jacob. Of these two, Jacob turns out to be a nasty character who needs a lot of work from God to make him into the third patriarch of Israel. When Rebekah questions God about the movements she felt in her womb, she is told that two nations are struggling there, and that "the elder will serve the younger". Later, Jacob seeks to cash in on this in two disgraceful ways. First, he cajoles Esau into giving up his birthright (25:29–34), then later when his father is on his deathbed he tricks him into giving him the blessing meant for Esau (chapter 27).

Jacob then has to flee from Esau's anger. We have the second sibling quarrel, after Cain and Abel, and before Joseph and his brothers. (With Ishmael and Isaac, the quarrel is mostly between the two mothers.) During Jacob's exile, God slowly reforms him, as Jacob the cheat is worsted by his Uncle Laban (chapters 29 and 30). Two encounters with God shape him further. The first happens before he meets Laban and marries his two daughters, who themselves are rivals for Jacob's love. He has a dream at Bethel of a ladder reaching up to heaven with angels going up and down. God renews his promise of blessing to Abraham's line, and specifically to "be with" this man who has had to leave his parents. This, in fact, is the blessing Jacob needs, not Esau's blessing, which was about wealth and power.

### Angels in Motion (Genesis 28:10–22)

> Angels are seldom absent,
> though not in need of ladders.
> We are, in our dreams at least,
> like Jacob, with the Lord beside him
> and the angels on the escalator.
>
> Jacob changed, a little; it would
> take a life of wrestling, famine
> and Egyptian family drama
> to complete his therapy.
> God teaches slowly, patiently –
> but keeps on moving,
> like those anonymous angels.

"Therapy?" said Jean. "Isn't that a modern word?"

"It may be a modern word, but the Bible is full of healing stories. We humans always need healing—from our faulty genes, perhaps, and certainly from what life throws at us. Some of us are fortunate enough to experience a lot of healing before we die, others have to wait till after."

"That's if you believe in life after death."

"Indeed," I replied. "And that took a long time to come to the surface. In the Old Testament, life after death is really about the survival of a people—and, of course, it is something of a miracle that the people of Israel have survived when so many of these other tribes have disappeared. Now, we all call Jacob one of the patriarchs, the founding fathers."

## Struggle

Jacob's response to the dream at Bethel is to say, "How awesome is this place! This is none other than the house of God, and this is the gate of heaven" (28:17). Bethel in Hebrew means "house of God", but "gate of heaven" is the meaning of Babylon in its language. At one level, the Old Testament shows us a struggle between the humble Bethel and the wealthy Babylon—where is heaven, where is God really to be found?

"Jacob's whole life," I continued, "shows how God likes to work through unlikely, even twisted characters. You see 'providence'—how God works out his good purpose in complex situations. And you see 'grace': how God forgives and does not deal with us as we deserve. In 32:10 Jacob prays, 'I am not worthy of the least of all the steadfast love and all the faithfulness you have shown your servant.' The Old Testament invites us to choose the way of humility, accepting what God offers us as a free gift."

"You've started to preach. Get back to the story, please!"

"All right," I said. "The second time Jacob meets God dramatically is after he decides to leave Laban in a hurry with his wives, children and possessions. This is yet another less than honest act, with no negotiation, and Laban pursues him. Two things allow a peaceful outcome. First, God appears in a dream to Laban and warns him against violence (31:24). Second, favourite wife Rachel, who has unreasonably stolen Laban's household gods, conceals them and tricks her father so that he is unable to find them (31:33–35)."

Jacob is now going to meet his brother again after many years, a meeting he dreads. On the road, Jacob has another encounter with God at Peniel, a wrestling match with a stranger who renews the blessing (32:22–31). Jacob is given the name Israel ("one who struggles with God", or "God struggles"). The story of this people is a history of struggle; their survival up to the present day again shows God's providence, and determination to see things through with people who are no more deserving than we are.

Denise Levertov has a marvellous reference to Jacob in one of her poems:

> Remember Cézanne, doggedly *sur le motif*,
> his mountain a tireless noonday angel
> he grappled like Jacob demanding reluctant blessing.[19]

"I love the way so many artists and poets use biblical characters," Jean pointed out to me.

"I think it's because these characters are real, flawed and in so many ways like us. When I read the Bible I'm reading about the politicians and people of our own age—and, of course, I'm reading about myself!"

The Hebrew of Genesis uses puns and word links. The name Jacob is the same as Jabbok but with two consonants reversed. The struggle by night, and the reference to Jacob's hip, both use words with two of those consonants. We have our own ways of doing this kind of thing in English poetry.

## Hip Surgery (Genesis 32:22–32)

No holds barred
as Jacob wrestled with the stranger.
He who grabbed the heel of Esau,
did a deal with God at Bethel,
got a feel for Laban's wealth
and lovely daughters, how
he's pinned at Peniel, and limps away
a humbler man.

No fix barred
as now we wrestle with the danger
of our easy days, and take our ageing
hips to orthopaedic surgeons,
get our broken limbs well pinned,
our fat flesh tucked and thinned
so for a price one walks away
a fitter man.

No space barred
to those who wrestle with the range of
figures that we conjure from the dark.
Before we cross the Jabboks of our age,
God, give us some such journey mark
as put the hip of Jacob out of joint
but left him humbler, fitter, and
a greater man.

"I see you treat the stranger as a dark angel, just like the *Zohar*,[20] which treats the passage as Jacob wrestling with his dark side," said Jean, who keeps surprising me with what she knows.

"I didn't mean to reduce the story to that—I just think it has a whole range of meanings."

"Do you know that Michael Symmons Roberts wrote a deep poem about Jacob's wrestling match?"[21]

"No, tell me about it," I said.

"It's called 'Choreography'. The angel says, 'I had to do your leg to settle things'. Settle what, I wonder?"

"A really good poet always leaves us thinking. It's never safe dancing with God. But it's good. '[Aslan] is not a tame lion,' said Lewis."[22]

Jacob settles into meeting his brother Esau, who turns out to be generous (chapter 33); he has even forgiven his rascally brother. Jacob then hotfoots it back to Shechem in the land of Canaan, still deceiving Esau to the last. He has now learned the virtue of restraint, but his sons have not, and chapter 34 describes a serious local conflict which leads to Jacob moving to Bethel, under God's protection (35:5).

## Older brothers

We have already met cases of sibling conflict (Cain/Abel, perhaps Ishmael/Isaac and Esau/Jacob). Each is different. The promised line of blessing continues through Isaac and his son Jacob, but there is what Jonathan Sacks describes as a counter-narrative[23] reminding us that just because one is chosen, that does not mean that the other is bad or condemned; even here there is a "both/and". As with Ishmael and Isaac, Esau and Jacob both bury their father.

However, sibling rivalry continues. As Simeon and Levi are tainted by their violence (chapter 34), Reuben makes a bid to assert leadership (35:22), no doubt realising from his family history that older brothers do not automatically get the first place.

## An Old Story (Genesis 35:22)

In that *ménage à cinq*,
full of ego impulse,
what would you expect
from Reuben, son of Jacob,
eager to assert himself,
test his manhood in
the most traditional way?

Rachel's death left Bilhah
vulnerable, youngest wife
unguarded from these men
with patriarchal ways.
Jacob heard, "was angry":
with his wife? his son?
or with his failure as a father?

"Did I ever tell you I had an older brother?" said Jean, during one of our meals together. We were in the Contini place under the National Gallery.

"No," I said.

"It was wartime, and my mother had a child by another man. She was ashamed, and before my Dad came back she got one of my aunts to bring him up. Later, of course, Dad found out, but they decided to leave things as they were."

Jean didn't seem to want to say any more at this point, so we finished our meal and went home. I emailed her with some more comments on the Joseph story.

Joseph, Jacob's second youngest son, is the one "set apart from his brothers" (49:26, looking back). But as we look at the amazing story of Joseph, through whom the chosen people are preserved, we find that it is actually through one of his brothers, Judah, that the story will continue, not Joseph's own children. Even though Judah is a flawed character who unknowingly makes his daughter-in-law pregnant (read the story in 38:15–26), this will be the family line that Matthew uses to introduce us to Jesus in the New Testament (Matthew 1:3). The heroine of Gen chapter 38, Tamar, is a feisty woman of "belligerent faith".[24]

## A dysfunctional family

The story of Jacob and his sons is well known through the musical *Joseph and his Amazing Technicolor Dreamcoat*. Joseph is one of several Old Testament characters who "prefigure" or model for us what will happen when God's own son turns up on the human stage. He is a precocious child who has dreams telling him that his father and brothers will bow down to him; he is rash enough to tell these dreams to his family, but remains his father's favourite, no doubt glad to wear his "gorgeous coat" (37:1–11).

One day the brothers get the chance to take their revenge. Instead of killing him, they sell him as a slave to some passing Ishmaelites (who are now wealthy!) and tell their father that he has been killed by a wild beast (37:31–33). Human trafficking, like rape, does not only happen outside families.

Joseph in turn is sold to an army officer in Egypt, whose wife falls for the handsome young slave; when Joseph resists her advances she turns on him and gets him put in jail. There, like the hero of *The Shawshank Redemption*, he earns the trust of the prison governor and ends up telling other prisoners the meaning of their dreams. This, eventually, brings him to the attention of the Pharaoh of Egypt, who is troubled by his own dreams. The upshot is that Joseph interprets Pharaoh's dreams, advises him what to do because of them and is promptly made executive prime minister of all Egypt!

While this is a dramatic enough story in its own right, the climax comes when Joseph's brothers arrive in Egypt during a time of famine, begging for food. Joseph recognises them, but they do not, of course, know this man who speaks to them through an interpreter (even though Joseph knows exactly what they are saying). This scenario is played out in such a way that the brothers are made to experience themselves something of what Joseph went through, and only when their remorse for how they treated him has been well and truly tested does Joseph reveal who he is. The story ends happily with old Jacob coming down to live with them all in Egypt.

### Hang in There (Genesis 40 and 41)

The butcher, the baker, the candlestick-maker . . .
no, not a single fable but a pair of futures,
a butler's dream, a baker's nightmare.

They hanged the baker, kept the butler.
Timing now is everything; a two year memory lapse
left Joseph hanging, deep inside his prison.

Two royal dreams then charted boom and bust
for Egypt, and the Middle East economy.
Such forecasts do not hang like fate,

but need a wise and waiting man
who knows the underside of life, and God.
Pharaoh hung on Joseph's words: the rest is history.

"The rest may be history, but I'm not sure that bit was. The whole story seems too good to be true. And it's constructed around those dreams," said Jean. "Doesn't that show it was made up?"

"Opinion ranges from believing that this is a pretty exact historical account to believing that no such person as Joseph ever existed. Scholars have widely different views. There's no way of proving exactly what happened, but there are two questions I would want to ask any scholar before I took their views seriously:

1. Are you open to the possibility that there might be a God who could be involved in our history in this kind of way? Or at least, do you agree that sometimes truth is stranger than fiction?

2. Do you understand the importance of dreams, especially in the non-western world?"

Dreams are undervalued in the western world, probably for at least three reasons:

- we think that all dreams are merely the brain sorting itself out overnight
- we relegate them to the province of therapists "who specialise in that sort of thing"
- we have lost any sense that God might communicate in this way, as part of the secularisation of the western mind

It would be good for westerners to hear how dreams are experienced in Asia and Africa and the Middle East, not least by the frequent testimony that people have come to faith through meeting a figure like Jesus in a dream.[25]

"That really takes us to the end of Genesis," I said to Jean, "but this whole thing started because I began to write a poem about each book of the Bible. Then I realised that no publisher would handle such an odd project—neither fish nor fowl, and bookshops like to know how to classify books. In fact, unless you know the Bible reasonably well, many of the poems may not make sense. So that was when I started writing lots of poems about each book, concentrating on particular stories—generally that makes more accessible poetry."

"Now we've been through the book, maybe I could follow your poem about Genesis as a whole—if you still have it."

"By all means. But I'll still give you an overview of Genesis to introduce it."

And this is how I came to include a poem called "The Journey", after the following overview.

# An overview of Genesis

Science sees things "from below", theology "from above" (hence the yin and yang of the second poem in the book). Science will tell us that *homo sapiens* is different from earlier types of human because of the size of our brains.[26] Theology explores what it means for *homo sapiens* to be made in God's image. We learn to think about everything from earthworms to moonbeams in this double way, without turning science into philosophy or reducing theology to poetry.

Genesis then moves on closer to everyday life as we know it. Abraham and Joseph are given the most space in the book of Genesis. Unlike many heroes in ancient cultures, neither is perfect. Abraham treats his wife badly, no doubt reasoning selfishly that what she needed above all was for him to stay alive. Joseph gets so much power that he seems to claim it for himself (44:15), and the way he got land for Pharaoh (and himself) in 47:13–26 was to come back generations later to haunt his descendants, who were entirely dependent on Pharaoh's generosity (47:1–11).

The book ends with Jacob blessing Joseph's two children (yet again reversing the order, chapter 48); then blessing his own twelve sons, making Judah the leader (chapter 49); this is followed by his death and burial. After that, Joseph has again to reassure his brothers, and by this time he is back to his humbler self: "Am I in the place of God? Even though you intended to do me harm, God intended it for good . . ." (50:19).

While there is much in the life of Joseph and his father Jacob which mirrors the need for us to revisit the scenes of old hurts in mind and spirit if not in place, in line with the insights of modern psychotherapy, the main intention is clearly to show God's providence at work, weaving hard times and difficult circumstances into his good purpose. It leaves us hopeful that even the worst situations and the worst people are capable of redemption and transformation.

Scholars argue over how far these tales are a record of what happened, and how far stories written to make a theology out of the sources available. On the one hand, there is less archaeological evidence (some would say none) to support these events than was once supposed. On the other hand, there is a greater respect for oral tradition (on which obviously much of Genesis is based). Certainly the Jewish scribes in Babylon who first drew together these documents treated all these characters as real people, and believers ever since have been humble and happy to regard themselves as children of Abraham and "heirs according to the promise".[27]

When we face critical times for ourselves and for other people, it will not matter what precise line we take about how these stories came into the book called Genesis. What will matter is how far we have let these words shape our lives and our obedience to God. If humans are to live as Genesis teaches they were made to live, the useful "both/and" criterion for understanding should be extended to bring together head knowledge and life practice as well.

The particular human project which starts in chapter 12 with Abraham is set in the context of God's purpose for all things and all people, shown by those two wonderful creation stories in the opening chapters of Genesis. The final poem tries to show this.

"Grace" comes into the poem. It describes the way God takes the initiative to sort us out when we can't do it for ourselves, and don't deserve it anyway. It is the root of our hope in a world which may sometimes seem cruel, without meaning and on the road to extinction. "Covenant" is what results when God says "I'm committed to you, whatever happens"—a bit like two people getting married when each promises to love "as long as we both shall live".

## The Journey (The Book of Genesis)

Colour painted prologue, theology in pictures,
a less than usual week, and wonderful
to spell it out in seven days of new
poetic praxis, novel history by the God
of Abraham (and every one of us), who
then is picked up in a patchwork promise,
made and remade to a homeless Hebrew.

*Homo* here is great, but not so *sapient*;
called to lead and care for everything,
the man, the woman, fail themselves
and God. The garden moves to memory,
the dialogue turns sour; the human delves
into a ground of being far more complex
than it might have been; we jail ourselves.

Hold the image, Adam! Hold the likeness,
Eve! Don't follow Cain, just be like Noah.
Maybe choose the bits you like, and frown
at Abraham welching on his wife in Egypt,[28]
or Jacob's sons' revenge in Shechem town?[29]
However, this is covenant stuff, God takes
the lead; it's grace, grace, all the way down.

Numbers count. Twos and threes, sevens,
forties, and of course the tribes are twelve,
old Israel's sons. Old Israel's struggle they laid
out on Jewish canvas for the Gentile world.
Four against five is local politics,[30] played
out to link Jerusalem with journey's
end: a running metaphor well made.

Study Joseph, modelling the greater journey
taken by a greater son of Jacob. Follow Joseph
into Egypt, wasting youth, tasting shame,
keeping nothing but his faith. Think of Joseph,
waiting through the years of wearing blame
unjustly on his soul and body. Look at Joseph,
when he got the chance to clear his name!

Resurrection to his father: and for us a mighty
foreword to the story of the Scriptures, more
creation out of nothing, meaning out of nonsense,
order out of chaos. We need Spirit, we need
God, we need Word and Light and Presence
showing—oh, divine community[31] at work already,
loving, knowing, telling in a past and future tense.

# Notes

[1] The name is probably from one of Abraham's ancestors, Eber (11:14).

[2] See Jonathan Sacks, *Covenant and Conversation: Genesis* (Maggid, 2009), pp. 71, 77–80.

[3] George Bernard Shaw, *Saint Joan: A Chronicle Play in Six Scenes and an Epilogue* (Penguin Classics new ed., 2001).

[4] See Hebrews 7 (in the New Testament).

[5] Psalm 122:6.

[6] Michael O'Siadhail, *One Crimson Thread* (Bloodaxe Books, 2015).

[7] Isaiah 49:6.

[8] See Genesis 12:2; 12:7; 15:5; 15:18–21; 17:7–8.

[9] This regards the Balfour Declaration, and the subsequent establishment of the State of Israel, as null and void.

[10] Circumcision is to be on the eighth day after birth (which is when blood forms clots a different way and wounds start to heal more easily).

[11] Qur'an 2.127, 14.39.

[12] *Antiquities* 1.xii.4.

[13] A philosophical term for the study of what existence and reality mean.

[14] Principally using sexual violence to humiliate strangers.

[15] Cf. Deuteronomy 7:7, 9:4.

[16] The curious may wish to read Isaiah 19:23–25 and reflect on it.

[17] John Goldingay, *Genesis for Everyone* (SPCK, 2011, part 2), pp. 76–77.

[18] Vishal Mangalwadi, in his book *The Book that made Your World* (Thomas Nelson, 2011), p. 180, suggests that this inspired James Cameron's film *Avatar*.

[19] Denise Levertov, "For Those Whom the Gods Love Less", from *Sands of the Well* © Denise Levertov 1996. Reprinted by permission of New Directions Publishing Corporation.

[20] The Zohar is a mystical Jewish commentary. For more on Jacob's hip, see Gavin Francis, *Adventures in Human Being* (Wellcome, 2015), p. 201.

[21] Michael Symmons Roberts, "Choreography", *Corpus* (Cape Poetry, 2004).

[22] C. S. Lewis, *The Last Battle* (*The Chronicles of Narnia*, HarperCollins Children's Books, 2009).

[23] Jonathan Sacks, *Not in God's Name* (Hodder, 2015), p. 110f.

[24] Ronald Wallace, *The Story of Joseph and the Family of Jacob* (Eerdmans, 2001), p. 27.

25   Read, for example, *Faith Under Fire* by the "vicar of Baghdad", Andrew White (Monarch, 2011).

26   See Yuval Noah Harari, *Sapiens: a Brief History of Humankind* (Vintage, 2015).

27   Galatians 3:29.

28   Genesis 12:10–20.

29   Genesis 34.

30   Genesis 14.

31   This picks up various hints in Genesis, such as the plural of 3:22 and the mysterious visitors in chapter 18. For a deeper look at how the Old Testament prepared the Jewish people to understand God as "community", read George Knight, *Christ the Center* (Eerdmans, 1999).

# CHAPTER 3

# Exodus

Genesis is the first of "the five scrolls", or "Pentateuch".[1] It ends with Jacob's family rescued from famine by Joseph and living in Egypt. The next four books focus on the history of the people who became known as "Hebrews", from their time in Egypt through to their arrival at their promised land, and the final chapter (on Joshua) takes them into that land. Putting these six scrolls together makes a "hexateuch".

Exodus is the second of those scrolls. The word means "going out". Moses, child of Israel and adopted child of the royal house of Egypt, leads the people out of the country that Joseph had temporarily acquired for them, and turns them into what will be a new kind of nation, called to live under law and under covenant. How exactly these two ideas relate will be one of the great themes of the Bible.

I was a bit anxious about Jean, now I knew she had Parkinson's. "Don't worry about me," she said, "nowadays you can live with it for years." I had the rather selfish thought that at least she would be there to discuss the other chapters. But I didn't say that, of course. I just asked her what she thought about the book of Exodus.

"Most of what I know comes from one novel and several films," she told me. "If any of it is really true, it's one of the great stories of history. It's about race, it's about adventure, it's about empire, it's about survival, it's about religion, it's about everything except sex."

"You're not quite correct about the lack of sex, but the book certainly starts with a gender issue. It is the opposite of the previous distressing policy in China: girls are allowed to live, but boys die. And the heroes of chapter 1 are in fact two women!"

Things have moved on from the end of Genesis. The number of Hebrews living in Goshen has multiplied, and to a new Egyptian king (the Pharaoh), they have become a threat. We soon find the first instance of today's antisemitism. This ruler "who knew nothing about Joseph" (1:8) began to use these immigrants as forced labour, and put pressure on the two Hebrew midwives—Shiphrah and Puah—to kill the baby boys but let the girls live, a drastic form of birth control. But the two women refused, joining a long list of faithful women in the Bible.

### Celebrity (Exodus 1:15–21)

Some choose celebrity, some covet it,
and some discover it through faithful work,
like Shiphrah, Puah, feisty women
who feared God much more than Pharaoh.

No Facebook then, no Twitter feed
to make some instant fame go viral;
only a people who held their memories
safe for their surviving children.

Who and what will save our youngsters,
guard them when so many die
as refugees from war and famine?
Where is faith at work today?

Grant us all this midwife spirit,
saying no to powerful killers,
helping birth what needs to live
and grow without publicity.

"I do admire real modesty," said Jean. "I often find myself agreeing with those French cynics, '*Toute la modestie, c'est le désir d'être loué deux fois.*'"

"Perhaps the opportunity to become 'a celebrity' in the modern sense occurs more in civilisations on the way out. But don't ask me to prove that. Like you, I love seeing someone doing the right thing just because it is the right thing—and in the Bible 'fearing God' and 'doing the right thing' go together."

# Genocide lite

Pharaoh's next move was to kill all new-born baby boys directly. Aaron was three years older than his young brother Moses, so he had escaped— but Moses was hidden for three months before being placed in a basket on the River Nile. The move (whether planned or not) worked, as Pharaoh's daughter spotted the basket, heard the child crying and took pity. A girl watching, perhaps Moses' big sister Miriam, offered to find a wet nurse, and (of course) got hold of his mother.

Moses was then brought up in Pharaoh's palace. The princess at least knew who he was. Film-makers, needing a back story, assume that he became the friend or rival of Pharaoh's son, who ends up as the Pharaoh Moses has to deal with when the time comes to negotiate the exodus of Israel from Egypt. Be that as it may, Moses ends up leaving Egypt in a hurry when he kills an Egyptian who is ill-treating a Hebrew.

### Only a Baby (Exodus 2:1–10)

Only a baby, only a basket,
only three months old;
only a lonely Hebrew boy-child
crying in his river tomb.

Only a cuckoo, nesting in Egypt,
only a refugee;
only a shepherd living in Midian
waiting, while his God stays shtum.

"So you chose a Yiddish word for silent," said Jean. "Appropriate, I suppose. Jews have had a lot of practice at coping with the silence of God."

"As have we all. Remember, we see magnified in Israel what is going on for all of us."

"What exactly do you mean by that?"

"Well, we call Jews 'the chosen people'. Chosen to be a light for the world. I think of them as a headlight, showing us how to get our heads round good and evil, what it means to be called or chosen by God, indeed what it means to be human in all our greatness and vulnerability."

"So that is why you use 'only' in the poem—Moses, a Jew, a human being, may seem to be only this or that, but really every human being is more than he or she seems?"

"I like having other people to explain my poems to me!"

## To Midian and back

Moses flees to the land of Midian, where he marries the daughter of the local priest and leader, Jethro. There he stays, while his people continue to live and groan under their slavery. Finally, God breaks his silence. Out in the desert, at the foot of Mt Sinai Moses sees a bush on fire, and discovers it is holy ground.

## The Burning Bush (3:1-6)

Who notices the little signs
slipped into daily life?
The smile, the cry, the star, the sky,
the desert bush on fire?

Who turns aside with virgin eye
to look, and pay attention?
The joy, the pain, the flash, the flame
of angel wings on fire?

Who listens to the voice of God
when life is bare and dry?
It takes a Moses, and a call
to set a man on fire.

Desmond Tutu tells how inspiring this story, and the promise of liberation, was during the struggle against *apartheid* in South Africa.[2] God tells Moses he is to lead his people out of Egypt. Moses replies that he is "a nobody" (3:11), and that the people will not listen to him. God patiently deals with all his objections, and when Moses asks God for his name, is told that "I AM" is the God who will deliver the people. This rich text can mean "I am who I am" or "I will be who I will be". It sounds like the Hebrew name for the Lord, Yahweh, and for Jews today is just "the Name".

"If I was a believer," said Jean, "I'd go for something like that. I don't like people who think they can be chatty with their God."

I let that pass. In chapter 4 Moses is remarkably chatty with God, who does get fed up with him in the end. However, God gives Moses the power to perform signs, initially using his stick (chapter 4), and tells him that his older brother Aaron can do the speaking for him when he negotiates with Pharaoh. Moses duly bids his new family farewell and sets off across the desert, where he is met by Aaron. Again, there must be a back story here that we don't know.

Moses and Aaron gather the leaders, tell them their plans, and meet the Pharaoh of Egypt (chapter 5), who pays no attention to their words, except to make things worse for the Israelites, who now have to "make bricks without straw". The Israelites blame Moses, who takes his complaint (as he will often do) to the Lord (chapter 6). God tells him to trust the history, trust what God has already done; but "their spirit had been broken" by their cruel treatment.

At this point the narrative breaks off to give us the family record of Moses and Aaron. It's a dramatic pause, and the editor's way of saying, "This is our family stuff, remember it when life is tough."

"If that is a dramatic pause," said Jean, "Does that suggest that Exodus is scripted like a radio or television play?"

"It certainly reminds us that the great majority of people who have known this story have learned it by hearing it told, not by reading it in a book."

## Power struggle

At chapter 7, the story of the ten plagues begins. It is preceded by Aaron turning his stick (rod in the next poem) into a snake; the local magicians do the same thing, but Aaron's snake then swallows theirs. The story has turned into a stage drama, but the progression is clear: the first few plagues can be copied by Pharaoh's magicians, but soon they drop out.[3] Each time Pharaoh is initially impressed, but then he changes his mind and refuses to let the people go.

"That's not how the text reads," complained Jean, who was carrying out her promise to read ahead. "God hardened Pharaoh's heart. Pharaoh was going to let them go, but God stopped him. How's that fair?"

"Actually, for most of the plagues we read that the Pharaoh 'hardened his heart', but by the time we get to the ninth plague, it is certainly the Lord who hardens his heart (10:20). I think that tells us that a person can become so set in evil ways that change becomes impossible."

Some people try to relate the plagues to natural phenomena; for example, pointing out that occasionally the Nile does flow blood-red, with volcanic matter which kills all the fish.[4] But whether you do that to "prove" the Bible or to "explain away" the plagues, you are liable to miss the point of the narrative, which is about a "power encounter" between the claimed-to-be-divine Pharaoh of Egypt and the God of all the earth.

## Spare a Thought (Exodus 7–12)

Spare a thought for Pharaoh,
plagued by Moses and his God;
the mighty powers of Egypt
threatened by a home-made rod.

Spare a thought for Pol Pot,
dying under house arrest;
frustrated by the failure
of his lifelong bloody quest.

Spare a thought for Putin,
keeping neighbour lands in check;
the weight of mother Russia
hanging round his powerful neck.

Spare a thought for Donald Trump
and every other lad or lass
who rides the tiger of big fame
until it turns and bites his ass.

Spare a thought for Presidents,
Prime Ministers and Sovereigns
who rule a restless people
wanting shot of such high heid yins.

Spare a thought, and coin a phrase,
join an Aaron with a Moses,
make the words do marvellous things
before the door from Egypt closes.

That closure would not come till a bit later—indeed, all the way to the promised land, Egypt remained a symbol of "the old Israel", the people with a mind-set of going back to slavery. First, the door had to open, and this was the result of the last plague, the killing of the first-born in every Egyptian household from Pharaoh down (chapters 11 and 12).

"That's the bit I can't stomach," said Jean. "God killing all those innocent children."

"That sort of question is bound to come up every so often in the Old Testament. It's because God is seen as the one in charge of everything, so if anything happens, in the end God is responsible for it. Just as if the theory of evolution is true, then God is responsible for nature 'red in tooth and claw.'"

"And when Moses' sister sings about the Exodus, she says with glee, 'The Lord is a man of war.'"[5]

"We'll get to that. At the moment we're just about to leave slave city."

Before that final plague caused them to be driven out in a hurry, the people are instructed to keep the first Passover Festival, "passover" because the angel of death passed over the doors of the Israelites which had been already smeared with blood. From then on, the first-born are to be dedicated to God, and bought back (redeemed) with an animal sacrifice.

## The crossing

Chapter 13 gives the first mention of the pillar of cloud and fire that led the people through the desert wilderness. We are told in the Psalms that God spoke to them from it.[6] They are instructed to camp on the edge of the Red Sea. Literally, this is "The Sea of Reeds"; possibly the place of crossing was at the end of Lake Menzaleh, off the Mediterranean, although later the name was used for the Gulf of Aqaba; those who think it must be the Red Sea would suggest the north end of the Gulf of Suez, which is connected to the Red Sea as we know it today.

Pharaoh then again changes his mind and pursues the Israelites (chapter 14), who are terrified by his approach. Moses tells the people to stand their ground. The angel of the Lord with the pillar of cloud moves between them and the Egyptians; the sea parts and the Israelites cross but when the Egyptians follow the sea flows back and they perish.

Modern people, looking for simple explanations, often explain away these things. The pillar of cloud, for example, is the smoke from a brazier carried by a guide (the "angel") at the front, the pillar of fire is what it looks like at night. Here the "both/and" approach can be very helpful. Maybe there *are* simple explanations, but if so, that is just the way the Creator God loves to do it, as Christians will find above all when God becomes an ordinary human in the person of Jesus. The miracle is the rescue of the Israelites from Egypt, not any one aspect of the journey, extraordinary as it may be.[7]

After the crossing, chapter 15 has a poem sung by Moses and taught to the people, with his big sister Miriam singing the chorus and playing the tambourine. It's hard to get the spirit of this purely on paper—it needs dancing and tambourines (15:20)—but here it is as a kind of popular hymn:

### Sea Power

I will sing, I will shout, I will dance before the Lord,
He's my chief, he's my reef, I've no chance without the Lord;
I will sing, I will shout, I will dance before the Lord
who has blown with a tempest on the sea.

I can sing, I can shout, I can dance before the Lord,
He has won, he has done just the most amazing things;
I can sing, I can shout, I can dance before the Lord
who has thrown Egypt's army in the sea.

I must sing, I must shout, I must dance before the Lord,
His right hand's so strong and it destroyed all Pharaoh's power;
I must sing, I must shout, I must dance before the Lord
who is shown to be mightier than the sea.

"Would you really call that a poem?" asked Jean.

"I don't think Moses or Miriam were trying to write poetry. They just wanted to celebrate something extraordinary."

"So a hymn doesn't have to be a good poem?"

"Most worship songs are not good poetry. Just as good poems seldom make good hymns. While some great hymns have layers of meaning, like poems, they also need a basic simplicity to make them accessible, which a poem can do without."

## God is not tame!

Jean was obviously bothered about something else. I had an idea where she was heading. This Hebrew poem is not a nice gentle song about the "spirituality" popular in the West today. This song is raw celebration of a warrior God!

"Do you really believe in a God who enjoys drowning Egyptian soldiers?"

"The story doesn't say God enjoyed it—it certainly says he did it. That doesn't match our comfortable ideas of a God who is supposed to be able to sort out the evil in the world without being nasty to anyone—but people living under tyranny don't usually have the same problems with the story of Exodus."

We are tempted to tame God, to fit God into our categories of what is reasonable. We prefer to leave belief in a warrior God to, say, Islamic State, and so we "rationalise" the song in one of several ways, for example to say:

- This is a primitive belief which changes later on in the Bible to something gentler
- We'll let God be angry with the sin, but not with the sinner
- It's unfair to lump all the Egyptians together, but (thank God) the New Testament is about the individual.

All three give us an excuse to leave the Old Testament behind, on the grounds that "now we know better". A humbler attitude recognises our limitations, admits that God is bound to be greater than how we can imagine him, and appreciates that all these different images of God have a place in understanding how God deals with evil and with evil people. I cited Louis MacNeice to Jean: "We jump from picture to picture, and cannot follow the living curve which is breathlessly the same."[8]

Jean nodded, but I don't think she was convinced. I consoled myself with the thought that, in the end, the only person who can justify the ways of God is God himself. As a bit of comfort I wrote my own little poem to celebrate victory over evil.

### End Time Music (Exodus 15:1–20)

Give me a high trumpet, give me a low trombone,
Give me a fiddle, a flute, a sax with attitude,
Give me a Bosendorfer with a deep deep tone
and sing me the song of Moses and the Lamb.[9]

Those harps are just a symbol of the orchestra
of heaven, when the universe is jumping
at the judging of the tyrants, where the register
of justice needs the beat of the bodhran.

Add in cimbalom and sitar, bongos, bass guitar,
for these songs are universal, and the world
is queuing up to learn just how things really are
when that whistle blows, and time goes down the pan.

"Isn't that poem a bit self-indulgent?" said Jean. "Your escape from the real world? At least when the slaves wrote that kind of music they needed something like it. And time isn't going down the pan anytime soon."

"John Bunyan once said, 'If a man would live well, let him take his last day, and keep company with it.'[10] It's called practical eschatology. And we need to do that sometimes for the whole world. That's why the book of

Revelation puts together this Song of Moses and the victory song of the Lamb—Jesus Christ."

I could tell Jean was a bit uncomfortable. Maybe I *was* being self-indulgent. Time to move on.

## Health

After the song of victory, we come back to reality. Going through the desert is tough, and finding an oasis where the water is undrinkable is the last straw. Moses prays, and God shows him what to do about the situation. There follows a promise of healing, a new name for God, "The one who heals", and their arrival at a large oasis called Elim.

"There is a church called 'Elim' up in George IV Bridge, isn't there?" commented Jean.

"Yes, and as you might expect, they believe in Christian healing."

Health is a big issue for a group like this on the march. In these books about travelling through the desert, we have a number of clues to pick up, for example:

- Wholeness. Plagues often break out, and they are always linked to disobedience and division in the community. God, as the creator and sustainer of life, is seen (in the OT) as responsible for everything that happens; so (15:26) God promises that if the people keep his commands, he will not bring on them the diseases he brought on the Egyptians. A community that keeps its life together in God's way is going to be healthy.[11]

- Mental health. A complaining spirit is likely to be depressed, a praising spirit is more likely to be healthy. In 15:19–21 we read of Miriam's gift for leading praise. More generally, when people trust Moses and trust God, they are happier and healthier.

- Physical health. Moses was brought up learning the wisdom of Egypt, which included some knowledge of surgery and herbal medicine, along with quack remedies which would harm rather than help.[12] The instructions God gives him are not like these; and they include provisions like basic hygiene (Deuteronomy 23:12–13) and quarantine (Leviticus 13:46).

"I think a lot of that was behind the setting up of the NHS," said Jean. "It was part of a bigger move to make society fairer and healthier. Now it's just about money."

"And complaints. Though that's not new."

We found the Israelites complaining when Moses' first intervention to Pharaoh made things worse, another complaint when they were trapped between Pharaoh's army and the Red Sea, and now that theme will continue when they have no water, no food. So God sends manna, which appears every morning (except the Sabbath!) until they enter the promised land. While manna may or may not relate to an insect secretion which can still be found in the Sinai, its importance is that it is God's provision.

### Manna (Exodus 16)

Manna, mysterious manna,
falling on desert ground
and feeding God's own folk.

Manna, mysterious manna,
falling without a sound
to make God's people praise.

Manna, mysterious manna
falling quietly round
the Jews exiled in Babylon

until the book of Exodus
takes shape, words to astound
and feed God's hungry ones.

For bread, the people were given manna. For meat, a flock of quails flew in and covered the ground (as they do biannually on their migration journeys). The book of Numbers expands on this, saying that the quails only came when the people had started to complain how boring and tasteless the manna was, compared with the vegetables and fruit of Egypt.[13]

The manna was such an important sign of God's provision that a ration of it was kept in the covenant box (the "ark" in old Bible translations), a coffin-shaped container that was kept in the holy place, about which more later. In the New Testament, Paul used Exodus 16:18 to argue that those with much should share with those who have little (2 Corinthians 8:13–15), believing that this is how the manna was shared out.

## Water and war

Water has always been a key factor in Middle Eastern history and politics. As the community moves on, there is another water crisis, and Moses takes the problem to the Lord (as the people are talking about stoning him). God instructs him to strike a particular rock, and water gushes out for the people and their livestock.

"That's what Petra is like," said Jean. "I went on a tour, and the guide explained how the rocks are full of hidden water reserves. If Moses knew where to strike, he could easily produce water."

"Yes, those who are always looking for the 'how' of a miracle will focus on that. The Bible text is more concerned about relationships, among God's people and between them and God. At this place the people sinned because they could not trust God, and so they needed to put God to the test."

The next story concerns the Amalekites, who attacked Israel at Rephidim. Here is the first mention of the younger Joshua, who is becoming Moses' second-in-command. Joshua is to pick soldiers to fight, while Moses goes up a hill to watch. He holds up his arms, and as long as he does so Israel is winning, but when he gets tired, the Amalekites start to win; so colleagues Aaron and Hur hold up his hands, and Israel wins the battle.

## War Music (Exodus 17:8–16)

Hands raised alone
to strike
or pray
will tire
and fall
without support of friends
so don't
go out
to war
or play
the violin without a shoulder rest.

"Just what has playing the violin got to do with Exodus?" asked Jean with a definite lift of the eyebrows.

"Nothing," I admitted, "except that later on, Israel will learn that it is possible to go to war and win against impossible odds, simply by consulting one another and then putting musicians in front of the army.[14] But we all need shoulder rests, not just Moses."

Jean is not the only one who sometimes goes in for lateral thinking. Anyhow, after the victory Moses builds an altar and calls it "The Lord is my Banner"—another new name for God (17:14).

"I thought you said God was just called 'The Name'?" commented Jean.

"That's Yahweh, the special name for God which is used in some passages. When the general name El is used, it's often followed by another Hebrew word, like 'my helping stone' (Ebenezer)—which is where the name Elphinstone probably comes from—it's even closer in German." (Jean used to visit us at Carberry Tower, which was once occupied by the Elphinstone family.)

# Jethro visits

From war, back to Moses' in-laws. Much is left unsaid, or hinted at—but what we have gives so much insight into Middle Eastern cultures, insights which the West ignored in their hapless attempts to introduce democracy. Leadership is traditional, patterns change not by outsiders removing strong leaders, certainly not by assuming that everyone likes western democracy, but by courteous confrontation, as in this poem. Moses is married to Zipporah, and Jethro is his father-in-law.

### Delegation (Exodus 18)

Desert wires
humming with the tale of Exodus,
Jethro brings a delegation,
two boys and mother coming
miles to meet
father, who has been busy of late,
for leadership is all-consuming,
male business in those days.

Jethro, used to
scorpions, noticed Moses scuttling,
soothed the sting of his complaint
with such an innocent question:
"Son, what's up?"
"God's spade work, father-in-law,
judging cases, stopping quarrels,
telling them what God commands.

"Here at Sinai
I will brave the storms on top,
meet God in the lightning flash,
hear his voice in thunder."
"Right idea, son,
wrong way: you need to delegate,
share power, get some sleep,
spend time with Zipporah."

A guess, that last:
Scripture here is economical
with words that Paul would later thunder,
"Husbands, love your wives."

"I get the message," said Jean when I showed her that poem. "No one likes being told what to do, least of all someone like Moses. What works is when someone asks the right question."

"Yes, when that happens it opens you up, and then there is a chance that you realise you need to change. Jethro knew that. Even the great Moses got some things wrong—happy the leader who has people round about who have the courage to ask questions."

## Mount Sinai

At the heart of Exodus is Mount Sinai, then a wild mass of rock without the Bedouin café on the summit which today serves tourists from all over the world. No camel station then, no easy, clean-cut steps, only slabs of stone, electric storms and the voice of God, who earlier revealed his name to Moses as the one who was, is, and is to come.

In chapter 19, the people are warned not to come near the mountain, which is full of thunder and lightning. This has a different tone from chapter 24 where seventy elders come up the mountain with Moses and a core group of priests, and see the God of Israel seated on a "sapphire pavement" (24:10). According to 24:18, Moses spent forty days and nights up the mountain.

"Is this two different stories put together?" asked Jean, who notices this kind of thing.

"Probably," I said. "It happens quite often in the Bible, and usually we can learn different lessons from each of them. It's like relating to different aspects of God—God is bigger than any one take on him."

Numbers like 40 and 70 are often symbolic in the Bible: the Israelites spent forty years in the wilderness (time for "a generation" to pass away), and Jesus spent forty days on his mountain fasting and being tempted. The number 40 often symbolises a period of testing, and was the maximum number of punishment strokes allowed.[15] The number 70 is a complete number (being a multiple of seven); there are seventy palm trees at Elim

(15:27), the Israelites spend seventy years in exile in Babylon, and a good age is "three score and ten" years.[16]

"That's me," said Jean. "I was born in the last year of the War. I'm beginning to stop hiding my age."

"What a seventy-year period we have lived through—worthy of a poem, I think."

### War Babies

2015: platinum jubilee
for the war end babies, born
to somehow drive this life-long spree

of growth from rationing to plenty,
from keeping hens and shooting game
to supermarket trollies, seventy

years to run down social capital,
abandon post-war certainties,
watch their sons and grandsons whittle

inheritance down to the brittle bones.
Parties govern by referenda,
children live on mobile phones.

A promised land may lie in front
—or maybe not—but either way
most in the wilderness will die.

"Will referenda deliver a promised land?" asked Jean.

"We'll encounter one referendum with Joshua," I said, "but Moses wasn't interested in them. Law worked only one way—from God to the people."

## Law and spirituality

What Moses received from God were primarily the ten commandments (20:1–17) but also laws for social conduct (21–23) and for worship (25–31). Jean felt she was on familiar ground.

"This is what it's all about, isn't it? The ten commandments. Basis of civilised society."

"Most cultures had some good rules. What is distinctive is what comes at the beginning," I said to Jean.

These commandments[17] are prefaced by "I am the Lord your God, who brought you out of the land of Egypt", which is in line with Old and New Testament teaching that God takes the first step with people, God declares his covenant, and it is then our responsibility to live as God tells us to live.

Observant Jews seek to keep these commands, not least the Sabbath day of rest and worship, which starts on a Friday evening and continues till sundown on Saturday. Followers of Jesus continued to observe them, with the difference that the Sabbath day became Sunday (the day of resurrection), but not until the Roman Emperor Constantine decided that his empire should be Christian, in the fourth century AD, would Christian slaves have (possibly) had a day of rest.

The first command is about heart and life, the next three commands are about religious practice, the next five about social behaviour, and the final command (do not covet, do not desire what belongs to someone else) is about the heart alone.

### Boundaries (Exodus 20:3–17)

Look for the places without a boundary
   which might define them,
the gentle earth, the open heart, the sparkling river,
the light of heaven and the love-lit parts of earth,
enjoy them, live with them and bless them.

Look for the people without a boundary
   which might protect them,
the poor, the sick, the lonely, those forgotten, strangers
– no one should stop you being there with them;
desire those places, live there also, give, receive.

Because the law is there for bounded
   people and for bounded places,
and it sets its own right boundaries,
but for these others law is not enough.

"We don't need more law," said Jean. "What we need is spirituality. That sets people free, and legalistic religion just ties them down."

"Religion has certainly become unpopular in most of Europe," I replied, "although there are now a lot of people who call themselves believers but don't attend church. However, there is bad religion and bad spirituality. I want to see good religion and good spirituality, and I think they are stronger together."

Today it is commonplace to contrast so-called "legalistic" religion with so-called "free" spirituality. The Bible has its own critique of religion, especially in the Books of the Old Testament Prophets, and later in the New Testament, but it does see spirituality as a mark of good religion, and this was an ideal held by those who put together these Scriptures as well as by the great biblical characters themselves.

Jean had not finished. "Do you know Kei Miller's poem on Genesis?"[18]

"No," I admitted.

"He takes the one word 'let' from chapter one, keeps repeating it, sees creation as God giving us permission to do all kinds of stuff. I could believe in a God like that."

"Sure. But in the real world you need some limits too."

"Abraham didn't pay much attention to limits, did he?"

"He may seem to be a free spirit moving from place to place," I pointed out, "and Moses the man with the commandments always hanging round his neck—but Abraham built his altars, and Moses enjoyed intimacy with God."

Most of the detailed laws are repeated or developed in other books, and will be considered there. Many of the arrangements for worship are repeated later on in Exodus, and we shall return to them. All are concerned with spelling out what it means for Israel to be what Godfrey Ashby calls "an alternative society".[19] However, the detailed instructions for the anointing oil and the incense are given here only (chapter 30). The ingredients are very precise (30:22–25). It's interesting that in 1989 archaeologists found a jug with oil of this composition dating back 2000 years, in a cave by the Dead Sea.

## Down the mountain

After the exodus from Egypt, Aaron features mainly as the first and chief priest of the holy tent. With one big exception—when Moses is up the mountain and off the scene.

I asked Jean casually if she ever saw her big brother. "Not much," she said. I waited. "We don't have much in common," she added.

"Well, you did grow up in different homes, you told me."

"It wasn't just that. He got into trouble. Drugs. He had a bad lot of friends, they led him astray."

At this point Jean knocked over a glass. I still don't know if she did it deliberately. But I thought it was time to get back to Exodus.

The theme of complaint, interrupted by the list of commands, returns with a vengeance in chapter 32. The people grow impatient with the absence of Moses, and persuade Aaron to make an idol out of the jewellery the people brought out of Egypt. Aaron tries to compromise by saying they will have a festival to honour the Lord (32:5) but it all turns into an orgy of drinking and sex.

"God knew what was going on, of course," I said to Jean. "God pinned the problem on Moses—'*Your* people have sinned'—then tells Moses to go down the mountain. When Moses appeared suddenly, Aaron didn't know what to say. He blamed the people for leading him astray, and said lamely, 'I threw their ornaments into the fire and out came this calf!'"

Back on the mountain, God has offered to make a great nation out of Moses' own family. But Moses pleads for these fickle Israelites, just as Abraham had pleaded with God over the fate of Sodom. Moses even throws the reference to "*your* people" back in God's face, and points out to God that if he destroys the people as a whole, it will make public God's failure to achieve what he promised Abraham and Isaac and Jacob. So God changes his mind!

"God does *what*?" said Jean, surprised. "I thought that was the one thing that a real God would not do!"

"That is exactly what God loves to do," I said with some enjoyment. "God is always looking for a chance to draw us into this kind of conversation, so we get the message that God is not only a stern legislator and judge, but a kind father figure who is ready to forgive his people."

There is a parallel case of Moses (and Aaron) pleading for the people in Numbers 16:20–22. These examples give us a model for how we can pray for others to a God who (obviously) already knows what is going on.

### Big Prayer (Exodus 32:11–14)

What on earth can touch the cosmic soul?
Equations proving everything is well under control?
Energy that's leaking from some occupied black hole?

Suppose they're wrong who say the universe is blind;
Suppose they're off the mark who feel that fate's always unkind?
Listen to old Moses thinking God might change his mind.

Prayer is still a mystery—no formula will do;
it's heart stuff joining head stuff through and through;
an invitation from a cosmic God to me, or you.

At Moses' request God does not destroy the people—but sin on this scale has consequences: Moses breaks the two stone tablets on which the law has been chiselled, grinds the gold calf to powder which he mixes with water and makes the people drink, and then his fellow-Levites, at Moses' behest, kill 3000 fellow-Israelites, thus consecrating themselves as priests.

"But you said that God likes to forgive," complained Jean. "That bit really makes no sense at all."

"Maybe that is because we think of the individual, not the whole community. Western individualism, in contrast to eastern solidarity."

Strong stuff indeed. Often baffling to comfortable folk who know little at first hand of warfare, and also to damaged folk who know all too much of warfare. It tells us that God will go to any lengths to keep his people in the right shape to bless the world, just as he would go to extreme lengths in the person of the one whom Christians worship as God, Jesus of Nazareth.

## The face of God

"You got one thing right in that poem, anyhow," said Jean. "Prayer is still a mystery. It's the gap. Cosmic God and little us. Remember that film, *Bruce Almighty*, and the million filing drawers full of prayers he couldn't cope with when he took over the universe for just one day?"

"Well, the film showed us how Bruce saw things. How God sees things may be rather different. That's one of the things the Bible gives us, little by little. The God-angle. It's a long book, and perhaps we need that length."

"Mm," said Jean, "that sounds a bit like poetry. Slow down, and let the words do their own talking."

The Lord says he will still lead the people to the land promised to Abraham, but through an angel, as his closer presence would destroy such a stubborn people. Moses himself, however, we are told, spoke with God "face to face", though on another occasion (all in chapter 33) he is hidden in the cleft of a rock so that the Lord can pass by him so that Moses is not blinded by God's face. Such differences can be explained by the presence of different sources in the text, but also remind us that sometimes God comes as an angel, and sometimes God shows himself in his glory. All of us, even the great Moses, only experience a little of who God really is.

## God's Life Space

God, is there room in your life? Real room:
stuff we can talk about, like space and time,
spectacles, sparrows, even wheelbarrows?
or had we better stick to sober topics:
truth and goodness, light and darkness . . .
Darkness! What a staggered thing;
it holds our minds in sacred gloom
with Moses deep inside a rocky cleft
(for who can see the face of God and live)?
Darkness deep and dazzling: hidden optics
make god sense of each black whole,
shroud our hearts in holy mystery, and
weave new physics in that inner room.

"Make god sense of the darkness?" said Jean. "That's a bit like John of the Cross."

I was surprised that Jean was familiar with the poetry of that Spanish saint. Again, I had underestimated her.

"Yes," I said. "Psalm 139 puts it one way—even in the darkness you cannot hide from God—while John puts it the other way, that we should seek God in the darkness."

Moses goes back up the mountain, the "ten words" are written on a second set of stone tablets, the covenant is renewed, and some more instructions are added, including the command for the men of Israel to worship at three annual festivals.

When Moses came down the mountain (34:29) he was unaware that his face was shining.[20] He had to put on a veil, which would give Paul a useful analogy (2 Corinthians 3:13) many years later, and may also have inspired Psalm 34:5: "Look to God and be radiant." Millennia later Adam Zagajewski would write, "Poetry searches for radiance."[21]

## Furnishing the sacred tent

While the people do set out again, led by the pillars of cloud and fire, the rest of the book of Exodus spells out how the tent for worship should be constructed and furnished. It was at the tent where God would meet with Moses (and Joshua). God had already told Moses (25:40) to make everything "according to the plan I showed you on the mountain"—a text often used to challenge people to carry out a vision they have been given.[22]

People need time as well as space to worship, so chapter 35 begins by reaffirming the need for "sabbath", rest. While the death penalty is attached (and there is an example of an execution in Numbers 15:32–36), in later times this was not carried out. However, keeping the Sabbath became so important that detailed rules were written down,[23] and discussed further in each generation, to guide observant Jews. Even today rabbis are expected to give such guidance.

To get a full picture of the elaborate provision made for the sanctuary, chapters 35–39 need to be read along with chapters 25–31 (where Moses is given his orders on Mount Sinai). The people are invited to make a free-will offering of gold, silver, bronze, threads, linen, wool, skins, leather, fine wood, oil, spices and jewels. Two craftsmen are put in charge—Bezalel and Oholiab, one from the major tribe of Judah, one from the minor tribe of Dan. These are the particular things to be made:

- The tent, which required linen, wool, cloth, gold hooks, animal skins and leather. Its frames and cross-bars were made from acacia wood, with silver bases and gold rings. There were woven, embroidered curtains, with posts of gold and bronze. Further, there was a larger curtained enclosure which also required posts and poles and carrying rings.
- The covenant box (traditionally called "the ark"), coffin-shaped, wax made of acacia wood, covered with gold, with gold rings so it could be carried. It had a gold lid with winged creatures of hammered gold in one piece with it.

- The table for the bread offered to God, covered with gold, with gold rings and carrying poles of acacia wood. Also gold plates and cups and jars and bowls.
- A gold lampstand with three branches on either side, seven lamps, and tongs and trays of gold.
- The square incense altar, made from acacia wood, covered with gold, with its poles and carrying rings. Also anointing oil and the incense itself.
- The altar for burnt offerings, made from acacia wood, covered with bronze, along with the equipment needed, including a bronze grating which fitted halfway up the altar, and its carrying rings and poles.
- The bronze basin for washing animal offerings, made out of the mirrors belonging to the women who served the worship tent.
- The garments for the priests, Aaron and his sons. An elaborate "ephod" or breast covering, with different jewels representing the twelve tribes on the shoulder straps; a smaller "breast-plate" also with jewels, tied on to the ephod (about nine inches square). A single cloth robe which went over the head, other special clothes, and a turban with a medallion on it which was inscribed "Holy to the Lord".

"All that reminds me of medieval English poetry," said Jean.

"What on earth do you mean?" I asked.

"All the players are men!"

So I tried to write a poem about Moses' wife.

### Zipporah Reflects

Where did they keep those mirrors?
Did the Egyptian women pass over their handbags
when the Israelites left in such a hurry?

All those jewels—but no diamonds?
How can a woman live without the odd diamond!
I keep mine in an old saddlebag.

As for Bezalel, him with the pedigree,
where would he be without that wife of his, doing
all the needlework, the fancy stuff.

My man's OK, off the mountain,
spends a bit of family time with us; pity there's
no room for that in holy scripture.

"What do you mean, 'him with the pedigree'?" asked Jean.

"Bezalel? You get his 'pedigree' in chapter 31. The Lord said to Moses, 'I have chosen Bezalel, son of Uri, grandson of Hur, from the tribe of Judah, and I have given him understanding, skill and ability for every kind of artistic work'" (31:1–5).

## The experts

It is, of course, hard to envisage all this metalwork and carpentry and needlework being done while the people were struggling their way through the desert wilderness![24] And yet we even have lists ordered by Moses and compiled by the Levites (38:21). Happily, it is more important to learn whatever God may want to teach us from these documents than it is to know exactly how and when they were compiled.

"Following the Bible isn't always easy," I admitted. "No one, for example, believes that we should copy exactly what Moses gave to the Israelites."

"So does that leave us at the mercy of the experts?" queried Jean.

"I believe Bible interpretation should be a partnership, so that scholars serve the people, and make their work accessible to anyone interested, whether in a church or not."

### Experts

Exodus and expertise
do seem to go together:
Moses, Aaron, Bezalel
– they run the show together.

Quite a formidable team
with Miriam, Joshua, Oholiab,
skilled and gifted, called by God
to sing or train as leaders, grab

the limelight, occupy these pages
crafted into holy writ
by other experts, men of words
behind the scenes, who bit by bit

recorded saga, lists of names,
events and places, scraps of story,
worked it into narrative
that tells our sacred history.

So far so good: but what about
today? We have our pundits
– expert scholars all, and living
by these books—or just their wits?

Anyhow, back in Exodus we read that everything was set up and dedicated, and the dazzling light of the Lord's presence filled the sanctuary (40:34). All through their wanderings, the people could see the cloud of God's presence over the tent during the day and fire during the night.

Back in chapter 29, there is one short, momentous passage which is not repeated (verses 42–46), where God shares with Moses the heart of all this craft and ceremonial—"I will meet with you . . . I will dwell among the Israelites". This verb, used for "setting up a tent" in the midst of a people, is picked up in the New Testament, and used to describe the idea and practice of incarnation in John 1:14.

## The whole book

Exodus is the record of this momentous migration of Hebrew tribes, which included a period of toing and froing for forty years through the wilderness, two steps forward, one step back, as their hearts were still in Egypt. The crossing of the Red Sea, in the final poem called by its Hebrew name, the Sea of Reeds,—which describes an area at the north end of the Red Sea—is an event and an idea fundamental to Jewish and Christian belief and celebration. But the wandering and wondering, somewhere between the past and the future, is also characteristic of human experience, and so this final poem uses an old form, a very slow form, the pantoum.

"Look for the repetitions," I said to Jean. "Exodus itself is full of actions which are repeated. That's why I chose this form to write a poem about the whole book."

### Legacy (The Book of Exodus)

Their feet crossed the Sea of Reeds,
but Moses had to change their minds
right out of Egypt. Lesser breeds
might be content with all those signs,

but Moses had to change their minds;
he took off apron strings. The folk
might be content with all those signs
which broke the back of Pharaoh's yoke:

he took off apron strings. The folk
might soon forget the past events
which broke the back of Pharaoh's yoke,
but they, without a future tense

might soon forget the past events
which introduced the power of God;
but they, without a future tense
could not then count on Aaron's rod

which introduced the power of God.
He led them by Mount Sinai. They still
could not then count on Aaron's rod,
trust this present God, until

he led them by Mount Sinai. They still
cling to the past; instead, they've got to
trust this present God, until
he gives them bread, tells them not to

cling to the past; instead, they've got to
learn God's future, understand
he gives them bread, tells them not to
break the bounds: with faith in hand,

learn God's future, understand
who God will be. Now, can Moses
break the bounds? With faith in hand
he climbs Mount Sinai; God discloses

who God *will* be. Now, can Moses
really stand the pressure when
he climbs Mount Sinai? God discloses
what God wants; the crowd cannot then

really stand the pressure, when
their leader stays so long away.
What God wants the crowd cannot then
crack: they think of Egypt every day.

Their leader stays so long away
they grow more restless, wondering,
crack; they think of Egypt every day.
The mountain smokes, flames, thundering,

they grow more restless, wondering
if Egypt was a better home.
The mountain smokes, flames, thundering
a question mark at God's real name.

If Egypt was a better home,
think where God's faithfulness will get us.
A question mark at God's real name
might cast a doubt on Exodus.

Think where God's faithfulness will get us
– right out of Egypt! Lesser breeds
might cast a doubt on Exodus—
*their* feet crossed the Sea of Reeds!

"Writing that poem made me think how hard I find it to change my behaviour," I admitted to Jean. "After a lifetime I still struggle to pay real attention to someone talking to me for more than a few minutes."

"Yet you believe God is patient with you. I must say I do like the idea of a God who keeps—covenant, you said?—a God who keeps covenant with people who are slow to change."

"Of course, sometimes a Bible story helps people in their immediate situation. Gladys Aylward had to find a way across the Yellow River in China, in wartime, with a hundred children in tow! When she was desperate, she thought of the crossing of the Red Sea. And she did, eventually, get them across!"

Later generations would remember this story and praise God (Psalm 105) without any qualms about the Lord of heaven and earth taking sides in human battles. Later still, war against a human foe became the fight against evil. As an example, in the Talmud,[25] the angels wish to sing a song over the Egyptians' defeat, but God silences them with, "My creatures are drowning—and you wish to sing a song?"[26]

Exodus from slavery has inspired liberation movements. In the Gospels, "exodus" is a word which was applied to the way Jesus left the world. On the hill of transfiguration, Moses appeared to him[27] and spoke about Jesus' exit from the human stage. Paul later pictured Jesus as the spiritual leader behind Moses, taking God's people out of Egypt and giving them food and drink in the wilderness.[28]

The next two books continue the original story, from very different angles.

# Notes

1. If you want a thorough Introduction to the Pentateuch in one volume, try *The Pentateuch* in the Oxford Bible Commentary.

2. In the Foreword of *Go out and Meet God*, by Godfrey Ashby (Eerdmans, 1998).

3. Two of these magicians were later on named as Jannes and Jambres, and are referred to in the NT (2 Timothy 3.8).

4. See George Knight, *Theology as Narration* (Handsel Press, 1977), p. 58.

5. Exodus 15:3.

6. Psalm 99:7, and compare 1 Corinthians 10:1.

7. For example, an east wind blowing at 63 m.p.h. for twelve hours over the Nile Delta would create a land bridge two miles long and three miles wide (Scotsman, 22 Sept 2010), but the real wonder is in the timing, and in the meaning of the story.

8. Louis MacNeice, "August", *Collected Poems* (Wake Forest University Press, 2013). He is writing about the passage of a day.

9. Revelation 15:3.

10. John Bunyan, *The Pilgrim's Progress* (Oxford World's Classics, 2003).

11. There is a detailed study of this in S. I. McMillen, *None of These Diseases* (Lakeland, 1973).

12. Such as the use of donkey dung (full of tetanus spores) when removing embedded splinters.

13. Numbers 11:6

14. 2 Chronicles 20:21.

15. Deuteronomy 25:2.

16. Psalm 90:10.

17. The Hebrew for "Law" is *Torah*, and this word is used by Jews today for the first five books of the Old Testament, "the books of the law".

18. In Kei Miller, *There is an Anger that Moves* (Carcanet, 2007).

19. Godfrey Ashby, *Go Out and Meet God* (Eerdmans, 1998), p. 98ff.

20. When Jesus was transfigured (Mark 9:1–4) on another mountain, Moses was one of the figures who appeared to him.

21. In the poem of that name, published in *Eternal Enemies*, tr. Clare Cavanagh (Farrar, Straus and Giroux, 2008).

22   For example, by the missionary Amy Carmichael. In ancient Middle East religions, a mountain was often the dwelling place of a high God; temples and their furnishings were linked with the idea of a "cosmic mountain".

23   In the Mishnah, a third-century BC document of oral traditions (see also note 25).

24   John Goldingay's *Exodus and Leviticus for Everyone*, SPCK, 2010, explains sensibly how these books came to include such elaborate instructions (pp. 3–5, 91–2, 104–5, 186).

25   The Talmud is an important Jewish document, with two parts: the Mishnah, dated about 200 BC, which lists the oral law, and the Gemara, about 500 BC, which is more of a commentary on the OT and on the Mishnah.

26   Cited in Jonathan Sacks, *The Great Partnership* (Hodder, 2011), p. 254.

27   Luke 9:28–31.

28   1 Corinthians 10:1–4.

CHAPTER 4

# Leviticus

"My first attempt to read the Bible, as a boy, was a bit of a disaster," I told Jean. "As I mentioned, I soon got bored. And that was long before I got to Leviticus!"

"Well, it's not exactly a children's book, is it? No children's Bible would have Leviticus in it."

Those who lightly think, "I'll read the Bible through", quickly get bogged down in the religious ceremonial of the book of Leviticus. Indeed, someone reading through the Bible for the first time might wish to skip this book (and even the two following) and go on to enter the land of Canaan with Joshua. But there is more to Leviticus than meets the eye.

The name suggests that the book is about belonging to the Levites, whose special task was looking after Israelite worship.[1] It is the name given in the Greek version of the Old Testament, but the common Hebrew name is "And He Called" (the opening single word in Hebrew). It is also about Israelite identity, what it means to belong to this holy nation. If the first creation story was about God making the whole world as sacred space, this book is about worship providing a particular sacred space where God may be honoured, with the number seven again prominent.[2] Worship, especially worship together, requires ritual—things which are done together in a certain way—and Leviticus describes one such set of rituals.

### God's Hello

To read the Bible once a day is ritual,
be it a chapter, passage or one verse;
to read the Bible every day is special,

giving us a mind map formed to nurse
us through disease and doubt, provide
us with a blessing to undo the curse

of Adam's sin, a light, a virtual guide
through Genesis, through Exodus, and now
Leviticus, the ritual justified

by where it leads, by when and how
God welcomes us with more than ritual *ciao*.

"I used to hate ritual," said Jean, "until someone explained that without a bit of ritual no one would remember to brush their teeth. So I suppose religion needs it too."

"The question is whether it's alive or dead. That's partly a matter for the individual. But ritual is for communities—like going to church at Christmas time. I was amazed to see our church full of young people on Christmas Day; and I gather that is happening more generally in France; what a strange world we are living in!"

"It's like standing at a crossroads—or maybe on top of a hill with a choice of several ways down." Jean can be quite gloomy. Time to return to Leviticus. Ritual at its best gives people an anchor and a history, and with that you can face life and its difficulties more easily. Leviticus was certainly written by someone who loved ritual.

Chapters 1–7 describe a series of offerings,[3] each with its own purpose, in two sections—first:

- the burnt offering (1:3–17)
- the grain offering (2:1–16)
- the well-being offering (3:1–17)

- the purification offering (4:1–5:13)
- the trespass offering (5:14–6:7)

Then a repetition of some of this with emphasis on what the priest does:

- the burnt offering (6:8–13)
- the grain offering (6:14–23)
- the purification offering (6:24–30)
- the trespass offering (7:1–6)
- some other instructions for priests (7:7–36)

## Serious about sacrifice

It is easy to caricature all this as just a way to "keep God on side" when he is otherwise fed up with human mistakes and misdeeds. We live in an age when God, if he exists at all beyond human imagination, is assumed to be simply concerned with human welfare and unthreatened by human sin. Love, it is taken for granted, is tolerant. Leviticus, as well as common sense, tells us that this is a serious short cut (as any lover could tell you). If God is tolerant, it is because something has been done to remove the offence of human shortcomings.

"'God will forgive me. *C'est son métier*,'" said Jean.

"'It's his job?' Funny how we think of that being French when it came from a German nineteenth-century poet."

Actually, the God of the Bible is not as casual as that. God is not offended in the sense of being "touchy"—he is offended rather as fire is offended by what burns up in the flame. Love is not soft or sappy; the holy love of God is like a fire;[4] and holiness (being set apart to handle holy things) is a major theme of Leviticus. This is why humans fall on their faces when God appears,[5] and this is why God himself provides ways for us to approach, as Leviticus demonstrates—which is, after all, true love on God's part.

### Fire Safety 1 (Leviticus 9:22–10:3)

I am not used to much fire.
It is well tamed by Scouts.
It decorates the friendly fireplace,
it remains within the furnace.
If out of hand, it is in far off forests.

I keep fire away from God.
He cannot be trusted with it.
God has no fire safety certificate.
If I go to meet him,
I will carry a bucket of water.

God is not safe, or simple, and the Bible itself gives us different sides of God's character. Moses would speak with God face to face, but he also had to be hidden from his glory.[6] Those who know God know awe as well as intimacy. The Bible preserves a wise balance for us, which Paul would much later spell out.[7]

"OK," said Jean a little sourly, "I can see you like a balanced view. But aren't you doing what those folks in Babylon did with their raw material—rounding off the sharp edges, imposing your own order on things."

"That's smart," I said. "We all do that a bit. The way I check it is by thinking of other parts of the Bible, bits we haven't read yet. That keeps me in order, at least to some extent."

"Would you say that having someone else look at the text with you might do the same thing?"

"Jean, you are right on the ball today. That is exactly what you are doing! And that's why people need to worship together, check their ritual works for them, so it's not just something from the past."

Since animal sacrifice and cereal offering are no longer practised by Christians or Jews, it is tempting simply to give a nod to the historical context, and pass on. Hidden in the text, however, are some things of more than passing interest. For example:

(a) Sacrifice takes place at the entrance to the holy tent (1:3), that is, on the boundary between the human and the divine. The person making the offering brings his or her gift and the priest then moves it into sacred space. Later events (Leviticus 10, Numbers 16) will show how dangerous this place can be, and how demanding is the call to be a priest.

(b) No fat or blood is to be eaten, no yeast or honey is to be used. Blood, symbol and sustenance of life, is drained from the animal and thrown against the altar. Yeast and honey were associated with fermentation and therefore decay. Salt is to be used (2:13), linked with covenant (Numbers 19:18).

(c) The animal offered should be without blemish; only the best is good enough for God (3:1, 6).

(d) Individuals could sin and a community could sin. A leader could sin, and an ordinary person could sin. There was provision for all of these cases (chapter 4).

(e) The rich were not favoured. A poor person could bring two pigeons in place of a sheep or a goat (5:7) or even a kilo of flour.

(f) The fire (to consume the whole burnt offering) must be kept alight day and night—echoed by the instruction to keep a light burning all the time in the sanctuary (24:1). This is both a practical requirement and a sign that sacrifice is always required. Hebrews 7:27 and 9:14 (in the New Testament) allude to this in calling the sacrifice of Christ eternal.

"I'm finding this hard going," said Jean. "How would it be if I just comment on your poems while we are in Leviticus?"

"OK," I said, "I'm just glad you're up for that at least."

## Ordination

Chapters 8–10 concern the priesthood, at this point Aaron and his sons. They were set apart by ordination in the presence of the whole community, which involved pouring oil on the head of Aaron, clothing him and his sons in ritual dress and sacrificing a bull and two rams. Moses used his finger to spread blood on the altar, on their right earlobes, thumbs and toes. He took a dedicated loaf of bread, and put this with fat and the ram's hind leg in the hands of Aaron and his sons, for them to offer. He sprinkled blood on their clothes, and told them to stay at the entrance of the tent for seven days.

After that Aaron killed a bull and presented the people's offerings. Finally, he blessed the people. Moses and Aaron together went into the holy tent, came out and blessed the people, and the dazzling light (*shekinah* in Hebrew) of God appeared; a fire consumed the burnt offering.

### Fire Safety 2 (Leviticus 9:22–10:3)

> Strange fires of Nagasaki and Hiroshima
> have lit a fuse in human politics;
> we have slowed it down with treaties,
> sprinkled it with good intentions,
> but it travels, smouldering still.
>
> Our universe was birthed in burning flame,
> our solar system lives on starry fire,
> one day it will consume its energy.
> Is there a fire beyond all things
> that might rekindle hope, goodwill?

"I think I see what you are up to," said Jean. "You are saying that science deals with fire, that politics and war are obviously about fire, so religion might also be about fire."

"Yes, but I'm not just playing with that word 'fire'. I'm trying to take the idea of love and light as 'fire' seriously. When people today chant that God is love, they just mean that God is nice. Real love is tough, and dangerous, and always risks getting crucified."

God is a consuming fire—an idea which is found also in the New Testament.[8]

What makes passages like this in Leviticus unusual, perhaps unique, is the refusal to present a rosy picture. In chapter 10, two of Aaron's four sons make an offering the wrong way, and the Lord's fire burns them up. It is not altogether clear why this happens, though Moses says they did not respect the Lord's holiness (10:3)—perhaps they thought they could do something themselves that would be impressive (turning mystery into magic, maybe).

Aaron and his two remaining sons then continue with the work of the priesthood, but get something else wrong, and Moses is angry with them. Aaron speaks back to him, putting all this in the context of his terrible bereavement, and Moses realises he has been too harsh (10:19). Getting the balance right between strictness and tolerance is never easy, not least because different situations and different people require different treatment.

## Purity

The next five chapters are about purity. They cover different aspects of practical healthy living, which today are considered on their own merits, but then were part of a sacred network of life as God's people. There is a lot about what you can and cannot eat, which is not so much about safe diet but about clean diet, related, perhaps, to the significance of not eating from the forbidden tree (Genesis 3:17–18).[9] Though it is true that pigs (for example) pose a health risk because they can suffer from the same diseases as humans—before fridges it was said, "Never eat pork in a month without an r in it!"

Chapter 11 lists clean and unclean animals, with domestic animals providing a template for what can be eaten.[10] Creatures are divided into what lives on land, sea and in the air (as in the first creation story). Then come animals with carcases that make you unclean if they touch you (or a cooking vessel), and especially if you carry them.

## Insects and Evolution (Leviticus 11)

Why did God make spiders, wasps and fleas?
(I don't mind butterflies and bumble bees.)

No doubt, a selfish question.
Faced with locusts eating crops, mosquitoes
and malaria, even *culicoides impunctatus*
(whom we call the midge or worse), harpoons
we fling at God might need a better hook.

Leviticus is realistic, down to earth,
without ideal restrictions, banishment
of vultures, flies or other scavengers
—just a thought out regulation, helping
us to deal with difference:

For the Maker, probably, a good solution
when you work it out through evolution.

"Do you really think agnostics like me throw harpoons at God?" asked
Jean. "I do ask questions . . . and I suppose I am trying to catch God
out—or perhaps just catch his followers out."

"Questions are often thrown into the air," I suggested. "My idea is that
some people, some of the time, might be hoping that a question might
stick, and that like a small boat with a big whale they might be carried
away themselves, to some place they don't expect to get to."

"Whaling is supposed to be bad as well as out of date. Why tie a poem
to a blood sport?"

"Whaling was never a sport. It was a way of life—an occupation
providing food and fat."

"Well, at least we seem to agree on evolution. Though I know you
restrict it to biology, while I like to think of it as a model for human
progress."

Evolution, in America, has become a flashpoint of division among
religious people, since the Scopes Trial in 1925, even though many

Christian thinkers back in the time of Darwin accepted his research and his conclusions. In Europe it is much less controversial, but there is still confusion between evolution as a scientific theory and evolution as a philosophy—the latter is a very different thing, simply a modern version of the Greek Epicureanism, which was well summed up by Richard Dawkins in his advert placed on London buses: "There's probably no god. Now stop worrying and enjoy your life."

The idea of human progress has taken a bit of a knock in recent years. But Epicureanism is still the default philosophy of Europeans and Americans—the atheist view that life simply develops under its own steam as the random by-product of the chance collision of atoms.[11]

Leviticus is far from the hedonism of contemporary London—as are most parts of the world today. The next chapter is about the impurity of childbirth, where a woman is considered unclean for one week after bearing a male child, and two weeks after bearing a female child.[12] This represents an ancient male view of sexuality, and any modern view of ethics, Jewish or Christian, has to explain how this should be updated, perhaps by accepting that God revealed his will gradually in and through the culture of the day. In any case the impurity was not about giving birth as such, but about the loss of blood associated with the birth, blood being a key aspect of ritual purity (17:11).

## Disease

Chapter 13 is about skin diseases (of which modern leprosy is just one), how they should be checked and if necessary isolated by a priest. Fungus on clothing is included at the end of the chapter. There are a number of case studies. While we might want to say that the priest was also a medical social worker, his prime concern was ritual. A skin disease was not just a health risk, it made a person unclean before God.[13]

"Moses or whoever seems to have been preoccupied by disease," said Jean. "A bit like poor Micheal O'Siadhail."

"How do you mean?"

"That book you recommended. I bought it. All the poems are about his wife—but her illness was far more advanced than mine, I'm glad to say."

I was embarrassed, but the twinkle in her eye disarmed me. She needs that sense of humour. As did my friend Clifford Hughes, who had a distinguished career as a singer, headmaster and finally minister of St Mary's Haddington. In his 20s he was the sole kilted tenor in a choir of English Oxbridge students, and became known as "Hairy McKnees". When voice cancer struck later in life he wrote this limerick:

> A tenor called Hairy McKnees
> used to soar to top Cs with great ease;
> but his laryngeal "op"
> caused his voice range to drop
> to *basso profundo* low Ds.

Chapter 14 deals with ceremonies of purification, and then considers what today we might describe as dry rot in houses. To be considered clean again, a person must undergo "social death" and stay outside the camp for a period; then a bird and a lamb are killed, and finally hair is shaved, clothes are washed, the person takes a bath. These are symbols of death and resurrection.

The provisions for fungal growth in houses, like most of Leviticus, go beyond what is required for the journey through the wilderness, and it is not always an easy task to distinguish what comes from Moses, as the text infers, and what was filled in later on. My own view is that such uncertainty is part of God's providence, and that we are meant to consider these texts "as if" they came from Moses.[14] The Scottish biblical scholar Iain Provan says that if Moses did not exist we would have to invent him.[15] We still are left with the task of interpretation, working out what they meant for people then and what they mean for us now.

Chapter 15 concerns discharges of semen and discharges of blood (in normal and abnormal situations), with similar provisions for making people clean. The body and sexuality are placed firmly in the context of theology and ritual practice; there is no suggestion that intercourse in itself is unclean, rather a recognition that the sexual act is somehow at the boundary between life and death.[16]

Today we take for granted rules for good sanitation, and isolation of infectious cases (chapters 13 and 15). It was only in the second half of the nineteenth century that medical practice rediscovered the importance of washing hands in fresh water.[17]

## The Day of Atonement

Jean came back on board when I drew her attention to the 1973 Arab-Israeli War. "It was launched on *Yom Kippur*, the Day of Atonement," I said. "It's the most important day in the Jewish calendar. So the nation was preoccupied."

Leviticus 16 tells us about this Day, an annual ritual of purification for priests, place and people.

Following the killing of a bull, the unique part of the procedure is what happens to two goats. Lots are cast (like throwing dice) and one goat is sacrificed as a sin offering to the Lord; its blood is taken inside the curtain and sprinkled both on the lid of the covenant box, and in front of it; the blood of bull and goat is sprinkled seven times. This is the most holy part of all rituals, carried out by the high priest once a year.

The other goat is presented alive before God, the sins of the people are confessed over it, then a designated person takes the goat away into the wilderness and sets it free. William Tyndale, an early Bible translator, introduced the word "scapegoat" to the English language, from Leviticus 16:8. The goat is being sent to a mysterious demonic being called Azazel, perhaps symbolic of the chaos of a world without God's created order.

Then Aaron changes his clothes, washes his body, continues with the burnt offering of bull and goat, while the live goat-tender also has to wash and change. Finally the carcases of the bull and first goat are burned outside the camp.

"So you're going to write a poem about the Day of Atonement?" asked Jean.

"I think I must," I said. "But I want to connect past and present. *Yom Kippur* is so much part of Israel, whose modern history is as extraordinary as its ancient history. It is surrounded by countries that talk about exterminating Israel; so far it has survived against the odds. And what fascinates me about the Yom Kippur War is that the country was still caring for the poor during the Muslim Festival of Ramadan which fell at the same time."

"So where do you begin?"

"I think I'll use the theme of blood, crucial to the human body and to the wider human story. But I'd like to bring in other themes from Leviticus, because *Yom Kippur* is just one part of the book."

### Yom Kippur (Leviticus)

It's all about blood. Get used to it,
wash your hands and pay attention.

A pig is not a goat,
dry rot is not wet rot,
a woman is not a man.[18]

Blood is life. Respect it, sprinkle it,
pour it, throw it red upon the altar.
There is an offering for everything,
but Nabab, watch the fire you bring.[19]

Sort out your diet. Locusts yes,
lizards no. Cattle yes, camels no
– and certainly no centipede.
No lie, no grudge, no greed;
use honest scales, no interest.[20]

Love your neighbour as yourself.
Keep the festivals, and keep the laws.
Sabbath is for restoration, seven
times seven leads to silver Jubilee
and property restored, for land
and liberty are in God's hand.[21]

*Yom Kippur*, one annual holy day,
a day of prayer and fasting, was
the day that Syria and Egypt chose
to launch unholy war in '73.
"Kill them, do not pity them,
and do not show them mercy,"
said Egyptian General Shazli.

Sadat, prepared to sacrifice
a million men to terminate
the State of Israel. Assad,
resolved to strike the enemy
and "liberate" Israeli land.
Read the documents, understand.

During eighteen days of war
Israeli Arabs volunteered
their blood. Ten thousand
parcels gave the poor a hand
to mark the month of Ramadan.

Blood is life. Respect it, sprinkle it,
but do not pour it senselessly
on idol altars. Those who call
for swords, by them shall fall.

An Arab's not a Jew,
but Jews and Arabs, both
can be good citizens of Israel.

It's still about blood. Get past it,
Jew and Gentile, and defy convention.

"Why that structure?" asked Jean.

"Well, Middle East stories often have the climax in the middle, not at
the end, so I had the longest stanza in the middle. Short sentences because

of the strict teaching of Leviticus about hygiene, diet, just relations and sacrifice. It starts and ends with a two line verse—two sentences at the start, and then at the end the reference to 'Jews and Gentiles'. Even with this most Jewish of books, the Bible is really always about Jews and Gentiles, insiders and outsiders."

It is through this Jewish race and its story that we see ourselves, both in their achievements and in their failures. The Old Testament has hints of how the two come together, the New Testament develops this in a particular way.[22]

## Ritual and moral holiness

Chapters 17–26 have been described as "a holiness code". Chapter 17 tells the people of Israel that animals must be offered to the Lord at the holy tent, not in the open field—possibly to guard against following local customs of worship to other gods. Resident aliens are mentioned, reminding us that Israel has always been exclusive in a religious sense, not in a racial sense.

Blood must not be eaten, ever. Created life is in the blood, and it is blood that expiates sin, blood that makes atonement.[23] Atonement is a mystery. It involves death, and life; it is at the heart of Jewish and Christian religion; there have been many attempts to spell out its logic, but no single theory has been accepted as the last word on the subject. In the Bible, understanding does not precede faith and practice, they are all bound up together.

Chapter 18, on sexual relations, introduces a prohibition which has divided the western world ever since religion and culture got divorced—a long process beginning with the eighteenth-century "Enlightenment" and culminating with legislation allowing same sex marriage. Some of the chapter is non-controversial, for example the prohibition of incest, and some highly controversial today.

"Why can't Christians agree?" Jean challenged me.

"Well, I'm glad to say that they do have some basic creeds, like the Apostles' Creed and the Nicene Creed, in common. When they disagree, it's usually over how the faith relates to current issues."

I told Jean that in my lifetime I had noticed five issues of particular controversy:

- the issue of nuclear weapons, and behind that the larger issue of whether religious people can ever support war
- whether the truth of religion matters, or whether all religions are different symbolic ways of understanding God and liminal matters (matters at the boundary of life and death)
- the question of land in the Middle East, and whether today the idea of "a promised land" should apply to the State of Israel in particular
- so-called "worship wars", perhaps at root over the question of whether worship should only be along lines commended in the Bible, or whether anything goes as long as the Bible does not explicitly forbid it
- homosexual practice, which is condemned in Leviticus 18:22 and 20:13

This fifth issue has divided churches in the western world, and divided churches in the West from churches in Africa in particular. Behind the particular issue, the division is really about whether and how the Bible is normative for ethics today.[24]

"Don't you think God could have made the Bible a lot clearer?" asked Jean.

"I'm a realist. We have to deal with the world we have, not some other world. If God has trusted humans to understand and look after the world, then it makes some sense to give us a Bible that we also have to understand and learn to obey, even if the results are uncomfortable—as they certainly are."

"I suppose people with different backgrounds always interpret things differently—that's why we fight."

"St Augustine recognised this. Here is one of his maxims—'In essentials, unity; in non-essentials, liberty; in all things, charity.'"

"So how do you decide what is essential and what is not?"

"The best way is through some kind of conciliar process—perhaps those scribes in Babylon saw themselves as an early example of that, though we have no means of knowing for sure."

Things aren't always straightforward. Those scribes would have an agenda which might not always be the same as their readers. To say that the Bible is inspired is to claim that they shared God's agenda, or maybe that God accepted the agenda they had, and used it.

## Neighbours and neighbourhood

It will take many years before the question "Who is my neighbour?" receives a clear answer. Often it is simply "my Israelite neighbour". The prohibitions in chapters 18 and 20 are made so that the people of Israel should be distinct from the peoples of the land which they were about to occupy, distinct not just because of their race, but because of their behaviour. For example, 18:21 accuses these peoples of child sacrifice.

Chapter 19 introduces a wider range of commands, concerning economic justice, impartiality at law, treatment of slaves, horticulture, witchcraft, treatment of children and honest dealing. Like the tenth commandment, it touches on matters of motive and the heart. The injunction "no hatred" is followed by "reprove your neighbour", perhaps foreshadowing modern concerns about the danger of repressed feeling, but then comes the second great commandment, cited later on by Jesus, "You shall love your neighbour as yourself" (19:18). This is extended in verse 33 to the foreigner living in the land.

Care for the poor neighbour is not just an individual responsibility—it has to be included in the economic structure of the day (19:9–10). In an age when combine harvesters hoover up the whole crop, the poor require better provision than foodbanks.

This next poem was written looking at Worcester apples lying on the ground. The drowning of the boy concerned, Aylan Kurdi,[25] drew worldwide attention to the Middle East refugee crisis.

## Refugee Status

The apples lie unburied in the grass;
one side is green, the other red,
but colours fade when you are dead
and lying at sea level.

The waves delivered Alan to the shore;
his skin was dark, and mine is light,
but colours fade when you take flight
and end up at sea level.

The Parties wait, uncertain in the main,
one brand is red, another blue,
but colours fade when you are through
with lying at sea level.

So pick the fruit, unblemished, while you can,
one side is red, another green,
but colours fade once you have seen
we're equal at sea level.

"That's not a very Scottish poem," observed Jean. "English political colours!"

"Well, Jean," I said, "It was written in an English apple orchard!"

The odd command not to mix seed (19.19), or make a garment of two kinds of material, reflects the desire to keep the created order pure, not muddled up. For us, that issue might be put in a different way—does the way we practise land use and technology properly reflect God's creative intention for the world, which is more obvious when it comes to verses 23–25?

The instructions of chapter 18 begin with the phrase "I am the Lord your God" (as did the ten commandments), since all the laws are given for a people bound to God in covenant relationship. They are never presented as if they could provide some ideal way of organising human community life. Chapter 19 repeats the phrase after many of the commands, because in Leviticus, laws of holiness and justice go together.

The following two chapters concern the holiness of priests and offerings and end, again, with the rationale of all the commands: "I am the Lord, who brought you out of the land of Egypt." Exodus remains at the heart of Jewish religion, a model which also prefigures the heart of Christianity.[26]

# Festivals

The Sabbath is the basic weekly festival (23:3). The Jewish Mishnah (part of the Talmud, see note 16 of the chapter on Exodus) in its second section includes the Sabbath with the Jewish festivals, as chapter 23 does. "Sabbath" means "stop", and in Genesis 1, it is God who stops working, hence its meaning as a day of rest. Leviticus, however, also presents it as "the Lord's day", and thus a day to gather for worship. In Leviticus there are five festivals, the first and fifth lasting for seven days, the others for one day:

- Passover and Unleavened Bread (starting in March or April)
- Harvest (or Weeks, or Pentecost, because it starts seven weeks, fifty days after Passover)
- New Year (which begins in September or October)
- Day of Atonement (*Yom Kippur*, ten days after the Jewish New Year)
- Shelters or Tabernacles (starting five days after *Yom Kippur*).

The Jewish calendar is a lunar calendar, which requires adding an extra month every three years, whereas the common Gregorian calendar adds a day every fourth (leap) year. Two other festivals, *Purim* and *Hanukkah*, came along later.

The two long festivals are reminders of the exodus from Egypt— Passover week about the very start of the journey, and the week spent living in home-made booths or tents a reminder of how people lived during their wilderness time. The earlier harvest festival is about the offering of first fruits, whereas the Festival of Shelters comes at the end of harvest. Later on, rabbis calculated that Moses must have given the Sinai Law on the Day of Pentecost, so that festival came to be more about the giving of the Law.

### Shelter for the World (Leviticus 23:33–34)

On the first day of Shelters, they offered 13 bullocks,
on the second day of Shelters, they offered only 12,
on the third day of Shelters, they offered only 11,
on the fourth day of Shelters, they offered only 10,
on the fifth day of Shelters, they offered only 9,
on the sixth day of Shelters, they offered only 8,
on the last day of Shelters, they offered only 7:
70 in all, to give light to the nations of the world.

Seventy stands for all the nations. I wrote that ditty to describe what has been said to take place when there was a Jewish temple; [27] at any rate, the festival looks forward to the conversion of all the nations to the God of Israel and their gathering under the *Shekhinah* glory.

"I thought you agreed with me that Jews are not evangelists?" was Jean's comment.

"They leave it to God," I said.

"Even though he stayed silent during the Holocaust?"

"Jews like to use stories to discuss these things. Like the two rabbis who convinced one another that God no longer existed, and then reminded each other it was time for prayers."

# Light in darkness

One of the great Bible themes is "light". In the beginning God said, "Let there be light" and light appeared (Genesis 1:3). God revealed himself as light (the *Shekhinah*), and asked for a lamp to be kept burning all the time in his sanctuary (24:1–3). Holy places of all religions place objects carefully, and all require people who will do the everyday jobs of cleaning, hanging, lighting and welcoming. The next poem is a celebration of such people who do these jobs in homes, synagogues, churches, temples and wherever people gather. In the OT, the spiritual is not divorced from the everyday, and in Jewish custom education is practical as well as academic.

## Lamplighters (Leviticus 24:1–4)

See them hanging,
high above the tourists'
thronging chancels?
They sanctify with no sweat
save the running cost of oil
(or electricity to brave
the wrath of those who say
oil was enough for Moses
– so let it stay that way.)

See us banging
on about the Spirit
as the lamp of God
in human hearts,
relegating Aaron,
knowing that the last
word has been spoken?
All these worship lights
are just a token?

See haranguing?
Spare a thought
for friends who polish lights,
remind us that a glint
of what is past may help
a man to find his roots,
a woman yearning
for a faith that she can touch.
Keep house lights burning.

We humans have very different personalities. Some people come to prayer most easily through objects like candles which they can sense. Some like silence. Others like ideas which can be expressed in words. I started with words, and I remember mildly confounding the Iona Community leader George MacLeod who was preparing me for confirmation; he said, "What is your image of God?" no doubt expecting me to say, "An old man with a beard", "a stern judge" or something like that. Instead I said (far too smugly), "God is Spirit."

Often we come to God initially through things which are most natural to us, but later on we learn to develop our "shadow side", using ways which would have been alien to us in earlier life. In later life I have found it helpful to use silence and objects as well as ideas. When we use poetry we are, of course, bringing together concrete pictures of things, observation of life, and imagination.

## Jubilee

What follows in chapter 25 is preceded by "When you enter the land . . ." We then have an extraordinary extension of the Sabbath principle. Not only is land to be left fallow every sixth year—the use of fallowing being well known in agriculture—but after seven times seven years, there is to be a fiftieth year of Jubilee when all property will be restored to its original owner or his descendants. A trumpet is blown on the Day of Atonement for this radical year—thus tying economics to religious truth.

There is no evidence that Israel ever actually practised this. In the book of Deuteronomy, the principle is reduced to forgiving debts every seventh year. But the recent Jubilee Movement for writing off the debts of poor nations was inspired by it.[28]

"Left to itself," said Jean, "even a small local economic system will produce more and more inequality—how much worse it is today."[29]

"The growing number of people using foodbanks is just one sign of it. I think the current economic system is broken."

"After the War we thought we had found a reasonable compromise between socialism and capitalism, but it's not working like that today."

"I remember what Tom Mboya said in Kenya before he was assassinated. 'When we send students to Moscow they come back capitalists, when we send them to New York they come back communists.'"

Behind the command to forgive debt, thus introducing mercy into everyday life, lies a radical teaching (25:23)—all land belongs to God, owners are simply tenants (literally, aliens). This in turn has inspired many radical movements, from socialism to land value taxation. Whatever the merits of new campaigns like Positive Money, some way of writing off debt is becoming more and more essential. The poor are to be given interest-free loans (25:35–37). All this is because the land of Canaan was given to the Israelites as a gift, even though they did not deserve it (25:38 and Deuteronomy chapters 6 and 7).

Jubilee 2000 was a campaign that began in the offices of Christian Aid but became an interfaith campaign, supported by the likes of U2. Bono was doubtful if you could write lyrics about debt relief, but ended up saying that you could.[30] Here is a short poem on that theme.

### Jubilee Year (Leviticus 25)

We mark our jubilees with silver, gold and diamonds,
with a nod to rubies after forty years;
Here is a single stab at jubilee, without a single jewel
except the precious stone of justice for the poor.

Chapter 26 outlines the blessings of obedience, and the punishment that will follow disobedience, including drought and land becoming infertile, and finally exile, when the land will enjoy the fallow years denied to it. Finally, however, when the people are humbled, God will remember his covenant and renew his promise of land.

It is passages like this which make us wonder on the one hand, how much was "written up" during the exile in Babylon and, on the other hand, make us wonder at the foresight of Moses (who had, of course, plenty of experience in handling disobedience). In the modern West we sharply distinguish what is "written down" and what is "written up"; to understand the Bible we should hold them together.

The final chapter of Leviticus concerns vows, how to handle situations in which a person or an animal or some land has been dedicated to God. Various prices (valuing males more than females, notice) are set, with one exception: someone or something dedicated "unconditionally" (27:28–29) to the Lord cannot be redeemed, they must be put to death—a provision that will come back to bite one of Israel's future leaders.[31] Hence developed the later Jewish practice of introducing the evening service on the Day of Atonement with *kol nidrei* (meaning "all vows"), the start of a legal formula for annulling vows made rashly.

The practice of "tithing" (giving 10%), first mentioned in Genesis 14:20, reappears at Leviticus 27:30. While there has been plenty of discussion as to whether this is a realistic demand in the modern world, it remains true that often the last part of a person to be converted is their pocket, and the world economic order has managed to resist attempts to change it.

# Notes

1   The logic of this "covenanted response" in Leviticus is well described by T. F. Torrance in *The Mediation of Christ* (Paternoster), pp. 84–5.

2   This connection is explained in Frank Gorman's *Divina Presence and Community* (Eerdmans, 1997), p. 9.

3   For details and significance, read *The Temple*, by Alfred Edersheim (James Clarke, 1959).

4   Deuteronomy 4:24.

5   Deuteronomy 9:25.

6   Exodus 33:11 and 33:20.

7   Acts 17:22–31.

8   Hebrews 12:29.

9   See Nobuyoshi Kiuchi, *Leviticus* (IVP, 2007), p. 205.

10  Pigs are interesting, as they can suffer from some human diseases.

[11]   See Tom Wright, *Surprised by Scripture* (SPCK, 2014), chapter 1.

[12]   Goldingay in *Exodus and Leviticus for Everyone* (SPCK, 2010), explains that "unclean" means "taboo", not "dirty", and that the period was longer for girls because they would grow up to be child-bearers, involved with the mysteries of life and death (pp. 158–9). A similar argument applies to menstruation (pp. 155–6, and Leviticus 15).

[13]   Miriam, for example, in Numbers 12 is struck with a visible skin disease because she challenges Moses.

[14]   If we knew the answer exactly, we would be tempted to promote one part of the text over others; even so, the "class A text" of one scholar is often the "class B text" of the next.

[15]   Lecture to the Abbey Summer School in Edinburgh, June 2018.

[16]   *Divine Presence and Community*, p. 92.

[17]   S. I. McMillen, *None of These Diseases* (Lakeland, 1973), chapters 1 and 2.

[18]   Leviticus 11, 12 and 14.

[19]   Leviticus 10:1–7.

[20]   Leviticus 19 and 25.

[21]   Leviticus 25.

[22]   See, for example, Ephesians 2:11–22.

[23]   Hebrews 9:22 in the New Testament spells this out: "Sins are forgiven only if blood is poured out."

[24]   A recent thorough survey for educational purposes of the literature on this issue has been done by Paul Burgess. See https://www.scribd.com/document/224713487/Homosexuality-in-Church-Society-Mapping-the-Issues.

[25]   His family have asked that he be referred to as "Alan" in English.

[26]   Luke 9:31 refers to Jesus' death in Jerusalem as his "exodus".

[27]   See Victor Buksbazen, *The Gospel in the Feasts of Israel* (CLC, 1954), p. 49.

[28]   See www.jubileedebt.org.uk.

[29]   Read Katherine Trebeck, George Kerevan and Stephen Boyd, *Tackling Timorous Economics* (Luath Press, 2017), for a good analysis.

[30]   See Steve Stockman, *Walk On: The Spiritual Journey of U2* (Relevant Books, 2003), pp. 167–8.

[31]   See Judges 11:34–40.

# CHAPTER 5

# Numbers

My wife Margaret enjoys numbers—you have to, if you do Sudoku puzzles every day as she does. I'm more interested in the number of times the same issues recur in human history (one reason why the Bible is still so relevant). "Those who don't know history are doomed to repeat it," said Edmund Burke.

I expected Jean to enjoy studying this book. I was wrong—turned out she had taken a scunner at the collection of statistics. She didn't say why, and I guessed it was just the way education had been going before she retired. I didn't press it. "Why should we bother with all those numbers?" was what she said.

The numbers do bother some people. Chapter 1 lists the number of people who came out of Egypt with Moses, tribe by tribe. The numbers seem impossibly large (1:46, 11:21), and the three most likely explanations are that those in Babylon who edited the material:[1]

- either (a) they took a word used for a military fighting unit in its later meaning of "a thousand", which would make the numbers correspond with the much smaller populations of that early time
- or (b) read back numbers from the later time of the Monarchy (Solomon's time) to show God's marvellous care for so many people
- or (c) simply accepted the numbers that were written or handed down orally, for after all, we are talking about events which founded and formed a whole nation. The greater the number, the more the Jewish people could feel that *they* were part of all this.

The Reformer John Calvin was happy to make two different kinds of comment on the Bible. We should read it "as if it was written in the sky", he said in one of his Commentaries, but on the other hand he admitted that some of the numbers did not seem to add up. The Bible is not a modern book written for a modern audience that likes to check up on everything; it is much more concerned with why things happened than how they happened.

Some poetry was needed if Jean was to get back on board for this book. I already had a poem written about the whole book, but it was based on a pattern, and the numbers involved—so I went onto a very different tack (desperate measures indeed):

### Numbers

Numbers, I hate them.
They crawl like half-dead wasps
into the corridors of everyday life.
I won't touch them, they might sting
me into filling in a questionnaire;
they might creep over my wrist
and die somewhere in my sleeve;
then I would be responsible for
death certificates, reasons
why Bernoulli's model fails, and
all the facts of prospect theory.

Let numbers stay unborn, imaginary,
nested in some virtual algorithm
where some boffins get a buzz.

Happily, those scribes in Babylon had no such hang-ups. The numbers added up, based as they were on those twelve tribes. But the story still had features of a statistical nightmare: the journey from Mount Sinai to the land of Canaan should have taken them less than a fortnight[2]—in the end it would take them forty years.

"That's worse than the Scottish Parliament," said Jean. "In 1997 the estimates were for £40 million. By June 1999 the budget was £199 million. In November 2001 the estimate of final cost was £241 million. By June 2003 it was over £375 million. The building was completed in 2004 costing about £431 million."

I agreed, of course, wondering why Jean had made such a fuss about numbers in the first place.

## The Levites

Chapter 2 describes how the twelve tribes camp all around the holy tent, and the poem at the end of this chapter uses this structure to relate the book to the people of God today. Given that one of the tribes, the Levites, camps near the holy tent itself, the number twelve is made up by treating the Joseph tribe as two tribes, Ephraim and Manasseh. The Levites themselves are not numbered—a note of freedom in the midst of this ordered scene.

But first come six chapters (3–8) which seem to belong more to the book of Leviticus. They are largely about the duties of priests (descendants of Aaron) and Levites (the rest of the tribe of Levi). We are told exactly how the holy tent and its furniture is to be taken down, carried, and then put up again when next the people camp (chapter 4).

Jean sat up when we got to chapter 5. If that is possible in those deep Starbucks' chairs. "This is voodoo stuff!" she said. The chapter deals with "unclean" people, and includes the notorious "trial by ordeal" to establish (for a jealous husband) whether his wife has been unfaithful or not.

Clearly neither Jews nor Christians support such a biased approach today. What it shows us, however, is how even in a patriarchal society there was a recognition that if a woman came under suspicion, there must be some way of allowing her a chance to clear her name. This can be an encouragement to people living in such societies today in that, even if thorough reform cannot be achieved immediately, some small steps can be taken to make things better for women.

Nazirites (chapter 6) are a group who take a special vow not to drink alcohol, not to cut their hair, and not to touch a corpse. We meet this group later in the Bible, individually in the case of Samson and Samuel, and as a group in the book of Jeremiah. This chapter ends with what is known as the "Aaronic Blessing" (*The Lord Bless You and Keep You*), well known in various musical settings. These words have been found on women's jewellery dated around 600 BC.

Chapter 7 lists the offerings brought by the tribal leaders, one at a time over twelve days, for the dedication of the holy tent. The offerings included flour and incense in silver and gold bowls, and animals for the various offerings. Even though the tribes are by now very different in size (and authority), each one gives the same. What an encouragement to a Jew living in Babylon whose tribe (Naphtali, say) had been more or less wiped out of the Northern Kingdom of Israel, long before the same thing happened to the Southern Kingdom of Judah![3]

Finally in chapter 8 the Levites themselves are dedicated as a special gift to God. With a reference back to the final plague in Egypt, they are taken by God in place of all the first-born sons of the Israelites. The Levites, suitably prepared, are now qualified to serve the holy tent. They perform their duties from the age of twenty-five and retire when they are fifty (although in 4:3 the period is described as the ages of 30–50).

I went through all this fairly fast for Jean's sake. It's not the most interesting part of the Bible, even if it had its purpose for the Jews living in exile and wanting to understand their past. But it reminded me of an experience I had living near Nairobi, when I persuaded Rafe Kaplinsky to take me to the synagogue, even though I was a "goy" (Yiddish slang for a Gentile).

## The Living Scroll

This goy got taken to the synagogue
one Jewish Sabbath, all because
Rafe,[4] good neighbour that he was,
obliged, and drove us to Nairobi.

"You'll have to do a reading,"
said the leaders, "After all,
you're a cohēn."[5] To such a call,
Rafe surrendered, if embarrassed.

Men chatted downstairs, women upstairs,
with the service quietly rumbling
on. Then suddenly, the mumbling
stopped; a stranger grasped the lectern.

He'd come just then from Israel,
held the Scriptures in his soul,
sang the message from that scroll.
The angels woke, and wondered.

### The journey

Now the story of the wilderness journey picks up from the second year after leaving Egypt, with the second Passover, and what to do if you are either ritually unclean or away from home when Passover is due. The same law applies to everyone, whether native or foreigner (9:14).

The community move on at the command of the Lord (compare Exodus 17:1); a series of different trumpet calls are used to signal a gathering of leaders, a gathering of everyone, and the time to break camp (10:1–8). These two silver trumpets will be used in battle and at festivals.

The cloud and fire are first mentioned in Exodus 14, where an angel (the word means messenger) appears and leads them in traditional desert fashion with a burning brazier, giving off smoke in a cloud by day, and tinged with fire at night. But here in Numbers it is clear that God himself is leading them with a pillar of cloud and fire, right over the holy tent, and they only move on when the cloud moves (9:18–23).

"That sounds too good to be true—a kind of magic," Jean commented.

I was tempted to say that truth is stranger than fiction, but resisted. Instead I said, "I think the Bible shows us God, and ourselves, more clearly than we see them in ordinary life. So the good is very good, and the bad is very bad."

"That doesn't mean they don't need human help," said Jean, not too impressed. "I notice that Moses makes sure his brother-in-law acts as their guide." Hobab certainly features at 10:29–31. In this, as at so many points, God is preparing his people to understand the human and the divine as two sides of the same coin, which is, of course, how Christians understand Jesus Christ.

Sometimes we are given "models" which shed light across the whole of human life—such as the "cloud and fire" which led the people of Israel through the wilderness (noted in Psalm 44:3). So I used this metaphor in a different kind of poem, written from a window in Crieff Hydro looking across Strathearn to the Ochil Hills in central Scotland, which were wreathed in mist.

I was reflecting on how the nation of Scotland might be moving on. The Bible is a "model" book; meaning that when you read a Bible story it will have a fresh significance in every country and in every age. The challenge for any interpreter (or prophet) is to make sure that you properly "read out" God's message from the Bible story, as well as "reading in" your own circumstances. The latter can lead people to use the Bible simply to justify their own racism (for example), as the Boers did in South Africa when they identified the Xhosa people with the Amalekites.

## Cloud and Fire (Numbers 9:15–23)

Surreal winter cloudscape, three times layered
along the Ochils, cradling Sherriffmuir
as if to gentle history, and make
an overture in art to things impossible.

Take time and outstretched fingers, run them
carefully along those bars of fog, soft striped
dawnwear for the hills which know the time
to sleep, and wake when Spring unfolds, to
do the duty of each season; or maybe
veils, concealing futures languishing
in jails, unvisited since unimagined?
What season now for Scotland, what video type
of land is waiting to be brought to birth?
Stylish, connected, rich in mind—or just unkind?

What poet politician is there who will dare
lift off the blindfolds we all wear
and speak the words we cannot say?
What fire by night will match the cloud by day?

"How many politicians do you know who are poets?" asked Jean. I
hesitated. "Jimmy Carter and Barack Obama wrote poetry," she added.
"This side of the Pond, we have Disraeli and Churchill as writers, but
that's going back a bit. Of course they all write memoirs, but that's not
the same. In Europe, Václav Havel was a serious writer."

"Interesting parallel. Charter 77 and Moses staking a claim for freedom
from Pharaoh."

"Maybe," I said, "but here in Numbers the Israelites are wishing they
were back in Egypt!"

# Complaining again

Chapter 11 returns to the theme of complaint we found in Exodus—it was not an easy journey! Having complained about the lack of food, now the Israelites complain that eating manna is boring (11:6). Moses takes these complaints to the Lord, and God's answer is, again, delegation. In Exodus 18 it concerned judging disputes; now it is about others receiving a share of the spirit that God has given Moses. Their leadership is confirmed by a short episode of prophetic shouting (11:25).

Two of the seventy leaders were not assembled at the tent to receive the spirit—but they still shouted elsewhere in the camp and when Joshua objected, Moses replied, "I wish that God would give his spirit to all his people, and that they would all prophesy!" (11:29).

## In Praise of Shouting (Numbers 11:24–29)

Shout about this marvellous God,
have no doubt, just let it out,
throw his fame from East to West,
hurl his name from North to South,
stretch your throat and roar a note
of godly glee as antidote
to shushing, creeping, blushing, sleeping.

Let the Spirit take you over,
don't be shy, you will recover,
raise your hands and gaze at heaven
amaze yourself, you'll be forgiven,
call on Facebook all your fans,
amplify a thousand bands
with trumpets outing grumpets doubting.

Make it raucous, keep in focus,
open throttle, hold your bottle,
God deserves your best typhoon
when the Spirit storms at noon.

Along with the manna, God sent the quails mentioned in Exodus 16. Here the episode is given in more detail, including the epidemic (food poisoning?) that broke out. So far, all the complaining has been done by the people, but in chapter 12 Miriam and Aaron turn on their brother Moses, criticizing him for marrying a foreign woman (Zipporah has disappeared from the story by now, unless—as a minority of scholars suppose—Zipporah is the Cushite in question), and for taking all the leadership to himself.

"Something like that was bound to happen," said Jean. "Aaron was the older child, guardian of morals for the family. Moses was the tearaway."

I had a sense there was more to it, and waited. Sure enough, Jean went on. "In our family, it was the other way round. I was the guardian of morals—but then, Jim was my half-brother."

"You said he got into trouble?"

"He actually did time. Barlinnie. Wasn't even in Edinburgh. Strange thing was that prison seemed to do him some good. He found religion. Changed him, at any rate."

"So how much do you see of him?"

"Not so much. I suppose I was ashamed of him. He's in a home in Glasgow now."

I nodded. That was the Bible doing its job, I thought. Making connections for us. Though I wasn't sure how to pick up the threads—another time, maybe.

Anyhow, God summons Aaron and Miriam to hear him, and affirms that Moses has a unique leadership, in charge of all Israel and meeting God "face to face". Miriam is struck with a disease that leaves her skin white and Aaron pleads for mercy. After Miriam has been shut out of the camp for a week, things return to normal and the people set out again.

## The twelve spies

The people have reached the southern edge of the land of Canaan, and Moses chooses one from each tribe to go and spy out the land. The names are all recorded, with a note that the name of Hoshea son of Nun is (only now) to be changed to Joshua. This tells us two things:

- these records are old and well preserved in oral tradition
- there are different records, and the editors made use of different records without necessarily worrying whether they were exactly the same.

The spies are away for forty days, and bring back two conflicting reports—the land is very fertile, but is occupied by giants with well-fortified cities. As a result, ten of the spies say "We can't do it", while Caleb and Joshua say "Yes we can." The story is beautifully summed up in a children's chorus:

Twelve men went to spy in Canaan:
ten were bad, two were good.
What did they go to spy in Canaan
(ten were bad, two were good)?
Some saw the giants tough and tall,
some saw the grapes in clusters fall,
some saw that God was in it all,
ten were bad, two were good.

The people back the ten who lacked faith, and complain against Moses and Aaron. The *Shekinah* light appears over the tent, God repeats his threat to destroy the people and support Moses alone, and (as in Exodus) Moses negotiates forgiveness for them. The upshot is that God decrees that only the next generation will enter the promised land; this generation will die in the wilderness (except for Caleb and Joshua). The ten faithless spies are struck down.

In spite of all this, some of the people now try to invade the hill country of Canaan, without the support of Moses. It ends in failure, and the narrative takes a break at chapter 15, with laws about sacrifice already met in Leviticus.

It will now be a long time till the people reach the promised land, as the following poem recognises:

### That Journey (Numbers 14:33)

What a day and what a date
for Jewish calendars
even if we struggle now to pin
the century.
What a way and what a weight
to carry, Moses –
with all that catering so heavy
on the scales,
plus the fray and mental freight
of life in Egypt,
gnawing at them, pulling them
like nodding donkeys
off the way, into a wait
of forty years.

"Forty years," said Jean. "I know you told me that at the beginning. But that's a long time."

"Well, seeing we're looking at Numbers. It is just one tenth of the time Israel spent in slavery in Egypt, according to Genesis. Getting rid of slave mentality does take time. It was one thing getting the people out of Egypt—it was quite another getting Egypt out of the people."

I thought of the journey Jean Sharpin was on, and my own journey, and wondered how much time we had left.

## Tassels

The Israelites were told to make tassels with a blue cord for the corners of their clothes. These tassels would serve as reminders of God's commands. Religion in Jewish faith is not just intellectual but practical, and we remember by touch and by doing more easily than just by learning off by heart.

You are unlikely to hear a sermon on 15:37–40, but the Talmud has a meditation on the blue thread of the tassel:

> The tassel is blue;
> the blue is the colour of the sea;
> the sea is the colour of the sky;
> and the sky is the colour of the Throne of Glory.[6]

The spiritual person learns to "see God in all things", and such a meditation is a model of how a small thing can easily be linked to something or someone much bigger. Meditation poems are generally quiet and relaxing; here is a rather different poem on the colour blue; the first two lines are gentle, then the mood changes.

### The Colour of Sky

> Dreams, saltires float
> under blue sky thinking,
> but the ground is muddy
> and the glass is sinking
>
> as events turn tough
> and the forecast narrows.
> Roll up your blueprints,
> now a nailprint shows

where a crossed out will
and a cosmic curse
knocked the best man standing
into death and worse.

Red sky at breakfast is
supposed to be warning
that the calm won't stay
much beyond the morning.

Faith gets exhausted
when the sky turns brown;
nightmares flourish
as the dark drops down

and the power is off
till God knows when:
resurrection's hidden
from most dead men.

Can our energies last
till the storm is past?

"So you're into rap now, are you?" Jean's eyebrows said it all. I threw away
St Augustine's advice[7] and threw the book at Jean. "Don't tell me you've
gone all missy about poetry. It's a huge and wonderful tradition, with all
kinds of forms, from William McGonagall to Jorie Graham."

Both the sea and the sky change their moods. So do we, and this is just
one reason why we need a book which has many angles, many themes,
many speeds. And if poems are to comment on this extraordinary book,
they may well turn out to be from many stables and in many forms.

## Dealing with rebellion

One Levite, Korah, is joined by three men from the tribe of Reuben to lead another revolt against Moses, claiming that if the Lord is with the whole community, Moses and Aaron should not be set above them. They had left the fertile land of Egypt, but Moses had failed to lead them into the promised land. So Moses challenges them to a power contest, which ends up with the rebels being swallowed up when the ground opens beneath them. The whole community protests about this, and an epidemic breaks out which is only stopped by a ritual of purification (16:47) for those who have complained.

Why is complaining so serious?[8] Here are some reasons:

- It is a challenge to Moses' leadership (which was so crucial, not only in leading the Israelites through the desert, but in forming them as a new nation)
- It takes people into "What if?" thinking. This is good when you are dreaming of possibilities, but disastrous when you let it take your mind back to things in the past that might have been different; then it leads to depression, doubt and an inability to move forward
- It undercuts faith. The Psalms, however, are full of a different way of complaining—because when you take your complaint to God, you start to build faith again.

Here, as a further sign of Aaron's authority, Moses takes one stick from each of the tribes, plus another stick representing the tribe of Levi, and puts them in the Tent. The next day, Aaron's stick has budded, blossomed and produced ripe almonds (17:8)! Whatever we make of this, it brings the rebellion to an end for the time being.

"So Moses is backing up big brother," said Jean.

"Yes," I said, "As the Kikuyu proverb says, 'One little finger can't squash a louse.'"

"I wrote to Jim last night. Snail mail. I couldn't find the courage to phone."

"Tell me what happens," I said.

That got me thinking about siblings, how they get along or don't, and how Moses and Aaron and Miriam related to each other (remember chapter 12) ... just the latest in a series of siblings we meet in the opening books of the Bible.

### Behind the Scenes

Did Moses ever laugh? Did
Miriam joke with Aaron?
And what about the quarrels:
could Moses keep his hair on?

So many earthy questions,
for better or for worse,
smooth or foul our sibling lives
with blessing or a curse.

There follows chapter 18, more about the duties of priests and Levites and their support, since they are not to own heritable property. "I the Lord am all you need," says God to Aaron—in a passage which is the only example of God speaking directly to Aaron without Moses. In return, the Levites must offer God a "tithe of the tithe", one tenth of what the people give to them.

"I've got mixed feelings about that," said Jean.

"What, about tithing?"

"No, about what God said to Aaron. I think he needed Moses. I suppose I'm thinking of Jim again. He needs me—but I've not been there for him. I hope that God really is enough for him. Not that it's any excuse for me."

I think Jean just needs me to listen. She obviously wants to work things out with her brother. Meantime we pick our way on through Numbers—and, as it happens, through the National Gallery, seeing we had been there for coffee anyhow.

## Events and what they mean

Normally ceremonies take place at the Tent, but a red cow is to be taken outside the camp and killed. Eleazar the priest sprinkles some of its blood in the direction of the Tent, the carcase is burnt, then cedar-wood, hyssop and a red cord are thrown into the fire. The ashes are collected and kept outside the camp to be used in preparing "water for purification" after contact with a corpse (19:11–19).

After Miriam has died and been buried at Kadesh, complaints break out again—there is no water. God tells Moses to "speak to that rock over there" so that water will gush out of it (20:8). This is a slightly different narrative from Exodus 17:1–7, although it may be the same incident as it happens at the same place.

Jean was looking at the painting *Moses Striking the Rock*, by Francesco Ubertini. "I see that Moses was carrying that rod of his, so the painting must be based on the Exodus version of the story."

"Look close up, look at the expression on Moses' face. He is holding the rod, but he is waiting to see what will happen. It could be either version."

Here in Numbers, Moses is disobedient in striking the rock instead of just speaking to it; water comes out, but it would have been more impressive coming after a word than after a blow. The narrative also presents Moses claiming to get the water out of the rock on his own account (20:10).

"I like that word 'wilderness," said Jean. "It has more resonance than 'desert."

"Yes, 'travelling through the wilderness' has been a great theme for individuals and peoples. In the New Testament, Paul uses it in a particular way.[9] He writes of the children of Israel being 'baptized into Moses' by their experience of passing through the Red Sea, and then eating spiritual food, drinking spiritual water (from the manna and the rock)."

"Quite a metaphor!"

"Yes, he even says that the rock was Christ journeying with them."

That was the link for the next poem (in *terza rima* form, in case Jean thought I was plunged for ever into doggerel).

### In the Wilderness

Day by dry and dreadful day they stalk,
kicking the stony sand instead of Moses.
Night by cold and bitter night they baulk

at their tough pilgrimage, holding their noses
to a grindstone handled by a scary God,
a threat unless their leader interposes,

hands them down a message on the nod.
They think of Joshua and Caleb, wish
they'd listened, trusted, been less slipshod

in their following, become less foolish
in their faith which flickered on and off
like fireflies back in Egypt, far less selfish.

What they need to lift them from this trough
is someone who can come and really walk
at their own level, break this dark standoff.

Paul says he *is* there: the living rock.

Jean eyed me. I couldn't tell at first what she was thinking.
"I suppose I was expecting this, sometime," she said. "Jesus. He was
always the answer to every question at Sunday school."

"I never went to Sunday school," I replied. "But I think I'm happier
talking about Jesus as the truth, rather than the answer. He doesn't stop
us asking questions. But he sticks around with us. As he stuck around
with the children of Israel on that dreadful journey. Walking with them,
as Paul said in that letter to Christians in Corinth."

## Moving on in stages

It is not possible to chart either the route or the timetable exactly from the bits of information given in Exodus and Numbers. Enough detail is given for us to take the fact of the Exodus seriously. Incidents are described which have inspired music and art and poetry as well as wise living, and we can be thankful for this rather than complaining that Numbers is not history as it might be written in the twenty-first century.

We read of the death of Miriam, then the death of Aaron. Mount Hor, which is visible from near Petra today, has a chapel on its summit in memory of Aaron. At this point, the Israelites are probably heading north between the Gulf of Aqaba and the Dead Sea, west of Edom, having been refused passage by the route known as the King's Highway to the east (20:14–21). Another possibility is that they went up on the east side of the land of Edom. Amos 1:11 probably refers to the threat of warfare by their Edomite "brothers".

One incident found its way into John's Gospel in the New Testament.[10] The people are complaining (again) about their miserable diet. God sends poisonous snakes into the camp, people are bitten and die. They acknowledge their sin and ask for help. Moses prays for the people, then makes a bronze snake, puts it on a pole: sufferers can look at the snake, and be healed (21:4–9).

"That's a bit odd, isn't it?" asked Jean. "In Genesis the serpent is a symbol of evil. And snakes bite."

"In ancient times the serpent was a symbol of healing as well. Maybe also there is a yin-yang thing going on here—what is in one context a sign of evil becomes in another a sign of good, and somehow they fit together. Ironically, later in the Old Testament that bronze snake becomes an idol and has to be destroyed."[11]

Now close to the southern end of the Dead Sea, they send messengers to the Amorite King Sihon to ask permission to join the King's Highway north of Edom. King Sihon attacks them instead, but is defeated, and the same happens to King Og of Bashan.

Chapters 22–25 concern Israel's relations with the Moabites, who are terrified by the arrival on their borders of this horde of people with a great battle reputation. The Moabites are part of a wider coalition of tribes known as the Midianites, and King Balak summons a prophet called Balaam who has to come all the way from the River Euphrates a long way north. Balaam is asked to curse the new arrivals.

"Do you believe in stuff like that?" Jean asked me.

"Yes I do—and obviously a curse frightens people into believing the worst. The same thing happens when a father talks down his children, like: 'You'll never be any good at that.'"

"Balaam must have been a shaman—and not just a healer, but practising the bad stuff too."

"It's quite a story—and spread over four chapters, giving Balaam a lot of exposure. But he seems to listen to God and he does what God tells him, at least in this case."

Two incidents are given in full. First, God tells Balaam that the people of Israel have his blessing. Balaam is told not to set out and not to touch the fee on offer. But he does set out, eventually, and on the way his path is blocked by an angel, which his donkey sees and he does not. When he starts beating the donkey, the donkey complains that this is unfair, whereupon Balaam's eyes are opened and the angel warns him that if he goes on he must say only what he is told to say by higher authority.

> When we are keen but not on key,
> like Balaam, turning wonky;
> when we are blind,
> and thrawn in mind,
> Lord, send us a talking donkey.

Second, when Balaam arrives, he is taken by the king up a hill, the two men offer sacrifice, Balaam goes further up and receives a clear message from God not to curse Israel. This he tells to the king, who is naturally annoyed. This is repeated twice more, with Balaam ending up blessing the people of Israel and King Balak sending him home without any fee. Balaam's last words describe the future glory of Israel.

## Courting love and disaster

Revelation 2:14 in the New Testament refers to a Jewish tradition that Balaam, knowing that they could not defeat Israel in battle, suggested to Balak that an alternative policy would be to try and integrate the newcomers by inter-marriage. This would shed light on Numbers 25. Sexual union leads on to worshipping the partner's god—a theme which will recur later in the Old Testament.

Plague has now broken out, understood as the Lord's judgement on this situation. Zimri, a family head in the Simeon tribe, brings the daughter of a Midianite clan chief into his tent, as a public act of defiance, seeking no doubt to establish the new policy (25:6). Phinehas, son of Eleazar the priest, then takes a spear and drives it through the pair of them making love in Zimri's tent. The epidemic is stopped, and God commands Moses to attack and destroy the Midianites, which is carried out in chapter 31.

"Are you still worried by all this 'search and destroy' stuff in the Old Testament?" I asked Jean.

"Of course. But I'm trying to get the overall picture. Then I should be able to ask the right questions."

I was impressed. We were back outside the Gallery, and sitting in Princes St Gardens. It was May, and we could see a number of couples lying in various poses.

"You know," said Jean, "I missed out on all this. I was too strait-laced. A career was all we thought about in those days."

*What might have been* is not usually a wise road to go down, so I decided on another route. "Did you enjoy teaching?"

"I did," Jean replied. "At least until the last few years. And I couldn't have done what I did if I had been married."

"It seems to me you followed the same pattern that God took with Israel. There are bits in the Old Testament where love and sex are celebrated, but at this point there was strict discipline. God had a reason for dealing with Israel in this way, and I believe he was leading you also in a good way."

That was the first time I had tried to link God directly with Jean's life, and I knew it was a bit risky. But she said thank you, and we went on with Numbers.

Several chapters intervene. There is a census of males over the age of twenty fit for military service (26:2), and some instructions about how the land will be divided up. We are told that when the Israelites assembled in the plains of Moab opposite Jericho all the men listed in the first census were now dead except for Caleb and Joshua (26:65). One case study leads to the ruling that while property normally passed on from father to son, where there are daughters and no sons, the daughters are to inherit (27:1–11, expanded in chapter 36).

### Syrian Survivor

Three girls had died of hunger,
Amal before she was five;
Mohammed kidnapped and killed,
which left only four alive.

Nizar and Sayid died fighting,
Ahmed stepped on a mine;
she was the only one left
The only survivor of nine.

Who will speak for Amena,
who will give her a hand?
When the war is over in Syria,
who will inherit the land?

## Chance and God

"It must be hard to believe in God in Syria!" Jean said in response to that short ballad about a girl survivor.

"Yet it's Europeans who become atheists. I've often wondered about that. It's not the human default position."

"Presumably we accept that things happen by chance, while to others it's fate, or the will of God."

"Ten per cent of Syrians are Christians. It's certainly not a land of atheists."

"Well, I'd rather believe in chance," she said rather firmly.

"I don't see God and chance as opposites. This may be another of those 'both/and' situations."

The conversation fitted in rather well with Numbers 27. God tells Moses to ordain Joshua in public as his successor (verse 22), with the comment that Joshua is to depend on Eleazar the priest, who will in turn use the holy dice (Urim and Thummim) to learn his will. It may seem unsophisticated, but later a Jewish proverb would say (and I paraphrase), "You can throw the dice, one by one, but all in all God's will is done".

Jean and I had a further chat about the ambiguity of "will", which can mean so many things:

- What is provided, as in a legal will, which should be carried out to the letter (but might not be)
- What is probable, based on our past experience ("the letters will be delivered")
- What is promised ("I will go with you")
- What is planned ("she will be going to Glasgow tomorrow").

Chance can change all of these things, but if God is God, there is no good reason why God's intention should not be carried out. The story of the Bible tracks this from beginning to end, with Israel a key part of this.

Two chapters about offerings follow, repeating Leviticus, then a chapter about vows, which must be kept, apart from the ruling that a father or a husband has a veto over the vows women make—the sort of provision you might expect in a patriarchal society. But I was still thinking about "dice", and the cryptic comment of Albert Einstein that "God does not play dice". Soon I had a rather different kind of poem to share with Jean.

### Holy Chance (Numbers 27:21)

So: God does not play dice?

Think of those priests with pockets,
Aaron, Eleazar, even fat old Eli[12]
hugging the holy dice, hoping
that some holy luck might still
postpone God's vengeance.

Think of those priests in Japan,
Ferreria, Garrpe, Rodrigues,
hero-villains in that Endo
story, hugging the holy chance
of life beyond God's silence.

Think of the holy heart of God,
bleeding, torn and screwed
by a thousand evil chancers
playing dirty with God's dice
and trading on God's absence.

"I was expecting another verse," said Jean. "It's pretty bleak as it is."

"Poetry has to engage with that," I said. "We have to weep with those who weep before we have any right to offer a word of hope."

## Final chapters

At this point Israel is camped, nearly ready to attempt the final crossing of the Jordan into the land of Canaan. By this time, it seems we are no longer dealing with the unorganised rabble who fled from Egypt, but with a people who have an experienced army and a large number of sheep and cattle. In chapter 32 the tribes of Reuben and Gad negotiate the right to occupy land on the east of Jordan, which is good for cattle.

There is the unfinished business with the Midianites, whom Israel defeat in what is called a holy war, under the command of Phinehas (chapter 31). This may well have provided a model for the medieval popes and bishops, who often doubled as army commanders.

The battle resulted in the slaughter of the Midianites apart from virgin girls, and the loot was divided equally between the soldiers and the community, with a tax of items to be given to Eleazar and the Levites. In the battle, not one Israelite soldier was killed, and in recognition, the army officers gifted all the jewels taken to the holy tent.

"I said I wanted to get the big picture before I asked you about the slaughter," said Jean. "But maybe I need to do just that! As a modern reader I find this hard to cope with."

Yes, passages like this are distasteful to modern readers, though the logic is clear in the ancient context. However, Midianites are still around in the time of Judges 6–8, so they certainly were not all exterminated. Perhaps the battle is an "ideal battle", described to show the importance of wholehearted commitment? Or if it was a real battle, were there Midianites elsewhere who were not involved in it?

It does raise the question of how we interpret the Bible, a study known as hermeneutics. There are many approaches, to help us explore not only "what did this mean for Israel at different stages in its history?" but "what does it mean for us today?" There are guiding principles, like (for example) the Christian understanding that in some way the text will point to Jesus Christ,[13] but because we share our humanity with people of every age, we will find the same kind of issues of good and evil facing us in the Bible that we find today, although the specific ethical contexts we have met in these early books of the Bible are very different. We cannot simply "read off" rules for conduct today, but we can ask useful questions like:

- What is really going on here?
- Where might I find myself in this passage?
- What do I learn about God and his purpose for all peoples?
- What are the questions that arise for me out of this—and is there further light in other parts of the Bible?
- Is there a key text I want to remember?

I tried explaining some of this to Jean. Her response surprised me. "You keep making such heavy weather of all this," she said. "Why don't you just accept that people in those days, whether we're talking about Moses or his interpreters, hadn't always got a very good picture of God? After all, your Jesus was supposed to be the man to sort out things—there had to be something for him to sort out."

I didn't quarrel. We still need a lot of sorting out today.

Chapter 33 sums up the whole journey through the desert wilderness, and gives the names of camping places. The people are instructed to drive out the inhabitants of the land of Canaan and destroy their idols. In a graphic phrase, if they fail to drive them out, the remnant will be like "splinters in your eyes and thorns in your side" (33:55).

Chapter 34 details the boundaries of the land, with its four borders (one of which is the Mediterranean Sea). It will be assigned among the tribes by drawing lots. Eleazar and Joshua, with the help of one man from each tribe, will be responsible for this. In chapter 35 the Levites are to be allocated cities and pasture land, and provision will be made for cities of refuge; if someone kills another person accidentally, they will have to flee to one of these cities, otherwise a kinsman of the dead person is liable to take revenge. This does not apply in cases of murder: "Blood pollutes the land" (35:33).

"This book of Numbers is a strange mixture," said Jean.

"Yes—stories and statistics, census and ceremonial, blessings and boundaries, faith and failure. You might say that life is a strange mixture too. It's certainly not neat. But one of the things humans keep doing is looking for patterns, looking for meaning, looking for significance. For me that is because we are more than just evolved apes. The Genesis phrase 'made in the image of God' keeps me always wanting more."

## And to sum up . . .

"So what about that poem you mentioned? With the numbers! I think I'm up for it now."

"OK," I said. "But I need to introduce it. After the initial census, the twelve tribes were instructed how to set up their camp in four groups of three, at the points of the compass. So this final poem sets out four modern scenarios of church and world in like arrangement, and also reflects in its form the numbers 12 and 40. Within each section, the second verse picks up one particular story from the book of Numbers, and the third verse suggests a contemporary link."

This poem is more like a simple ballad, not unlike the book of Numbers itself, which is matter-of-fact: so matter-of-fact that we could miss the extraordinary things that God seems to be doing among these nomadic people struggling through the desert wilderness. The Lord is leading them by cloud and fire!

### Four Square Mission

*On the east are camped so many brothers,*
*Greek and Russian Orthodox, Romanian and others*
*holding fast to faith and nationhood.*

The tribes set off tangentially, one o'clock,
for Edom. Moses took his staff and struck the rock,
so Israel drank, and found the water good.

But God was angry with his servant Moses
for using human might instead of simple words
of faith to show his power: could be an issue
which repeats, whether with Putin or Ceausescu.

*To the south, the Africans are not content*
*with older orders. They will pitch their tent*
*across the shrinking cosiness of Europeans,*

mark the place where Moses' wife was born
– a coal-black Cushite, to his siblings' scorn
and racist comments about Eritreans.

So God was angry with his servant Miriam
and banished her, a week outside the camp.
Is that really long enough to rearrange
a nation's immigration policy, entrench change?

*On the west, Americans still think in*
*methodologies, with the money to ink in*
*the pencil marks of earlier mission.*

Moses delegated spirit to two men
right outside his regimen—so then
he might have set a new tradition.[14]

"Power devolved is power retained", they said
anent the Scottish Parliament. No way:
in Christ this numbering God gave up control
that we and every tribe might count as whole.

*To the north, the melting ice, the polar bears,*
*unusual eco-tribes, geo-political affairs.*
*How will we face the challenge of* res publica?

Moses chose twelve men to go as spies,
but ten came back just terrified, their eyes
on giants. Salute old Caleb, and young Joshua.

Four winds blow, and all the world is buffeted.
The figures count our doom, and who is comforted
with trial by ordeal (now, or as in Numbers five)?
Give us discernment, cloud and fire, to stay alive.

# Notes

1    Katharine Sakenfield, *Journeying with God* (Eerdmans, 1995), p. 24.

2    Deuteronomy 1:2.

3    A point made by John Goldingay in his book *Numbers and Deuteronomy for Everyone* (SPCK, 2010).

4    Father of the journalist Natasha Kaplinsky—his name is pronounced Rayfi.

5    Hebrew for "priest"—traditionally, descended through the father from Aaron; whereas to be a Jew, your mother must be Jewish.

6    See Aryeh Kaplan, *Jewish Meditation* (Schocken, 1985), p. 72.

7    Augustine prayed, "God, save me from the lust of justifying myself."

8    Psalms 78 and 106 rehearse the miracles of Exodus, and the complaining that always followed.

9    1 Corinthians 10:1–4.

10    John 3:14–16.

11    2 Kings 18:4.

12    1 Samuel 2–4.

13    A straightforward example of this is Paul writing about the Exodus in 1 Corinthians 10.

14    Numbers 11:24–29.

CHAPTER 6

# Deuteronomy

Although it is claimed that Moses spoke and wrote much of this book
(1:5, 31:24), it is clearly edited (1:1–5 and chapter 34). There are later
editorial comments (e.g. 2:10–12). Deuteronomy stresses the importance
of sacrifice at one central place (12:13), whereas Exodus 20:24–25 refers
to different sites for sacrifice. "Jubilee" in Leviticus 25:23 is just about
land, whereas in Deuteronomy 15 it is about debts. The early laws and
practices are being developed for later situations.[1]

"That doesn't surprise me," said Jean when we were discussing how
to start this chapter. "The same sort of thing happens with every subject.
People do original research, it gets written up, then someone writes
another book, then people write a simpler school text book and so on.
They're all useful, but put them side by side and they don't all seem to
add up."

This book has a simple enough structure: three discourses by Moses
followed by some addenda also linked with him. How it was put together
together is more complex, and perhaps explains why Deuteronomy
reflects both Exodus 20–23 and the particular situation of 2 Kings 22,
when King Josiah discovered "the book of the law" during temple repairs.
That book seems to be part of Deuteronomy (which literally means
"second law")[2] and may even have been "planted" by a school of Levites
anxious to draw attention to the failures of the nation and its rulers.[3]

Chapter 1 gives us another version of two stories we have met in
Exodus and Numbers. No mention of the advice of Moses' father-in-law
that he should delegate, and no mention of God in the plan to spy out the
land—here (1:22–23) it is the people's idea. Motives are seldom simple,

and (like good poetry) the Bible gives us different angles and speaks at
different levels.

### Editors (Deuteronomy 1:19–23)

Even Moses, honorary editor-in-chief,
the way it's told in Deuteronomy.
And why not? With reporters' notes,
some early drafts, a century or two
of faithful storytelling, the word pot
is so rich with memories of exodus,
travel, waiting, dodging about,
and all the fuss of failure—working
through that fear of facing giants.

By the time of Exile, I can see
them working through the night.
Early editions, later editions,
final editions, it's all there,
set down in sacred style for us
to see this way and that, to get
not just a single authorised report
but different angles, soundbites,
clips of holy non-compliance

with the Pharaohs and the Balaks
and the tyrants that would follow
them to hit the hearts and minds
of God's own people then and now:
words to penetrate those cultures,
touch the likes of you and me
who carry scary kitbags, wear
great holes into our hope. That's
why godly editors make sense.

"Thank you," said Jean. "I need a touch of hope, especially when I'm lying awake at 3 a.m., wondering what is ahead."

## Coping with failure

What an anti-climax. Here is the last bit of the journey, the final assault—only for the twelve spies to bring a divided report, allowing the people of Israel to follow the faithless majority (1:19–45). It was thirty-eight years before the people would return to that place of potential, coming at it from a different direction (2:13–14).

Was it also a failure of leadership? Numbers 20:12 indicates this in another context, but the wider story shows how leaders suffer with their people even when they themselves have a clear view of where God wants them to go. In 3:23–29, Moses begs God to let him cross the Jordan and enter the promised land, but his request is not granted; here, it is because of the people that God would not listen even to Moses. Moses has to accept his limitations.

One of the remarkable things about the Old Testament is how leaders are not portrayed as flawless heroes, as in the epic Greek tales. Homer's heroes, like Achilles or Odysseus, are exciting, but they are not models we can follow or learn from, like the men and women of the Bible. Nor do they change, as do Jacob and other characters.

This poem takes Moses as a starting point to consider our human destiny.

### Airways (Deuteronomy 3:23–28)

We reach for sky. We grab some air
to fuel our grand affair with destiny.
We soon deflate.

Consider Moses; first but not
the last great politician whose
career went flat.

Who let him down? The lack of faith
of those he led? His God? His own
high-pressured fault?

Someone to bleed our tyres, too high
with airy pride, is what we need
for safer travel.

If such a one were ever found,
who'd find a way to ground the sky,
we'd breathe again.

"What do you mean, 'ground the sky'?" said Jean. "Isn't that the old Scots way of pulling down anyone who sticks their head over the parapet? Don't we need some people who reach for the sky?"

"I suppose 'ground' does now have that other meaning of 'punish', in a parental context. Perhaps I should have written 'earth the sky'."

"And sacrifice the rhyme?"

I'm not good at giving up rhyme. It was comforting to realise that Deuteronomy is about failure as well as success. Such a text helps people like us who live in a mixed-up world where things do not always work out, just as it helped Jews returning from exile in Babylon, who had to live in a society which was very different from the time when Israel had its own king.

They also had to learn to relate to other peoples in a new way. Deuteronomy 2:34 tells us that every Amorite was killed, following their rejection of a peace offer (2:26–30). Israel was not, however, to attack the

Ammonites, the Moabites or the Edomites (their cousins, 2:4–5). John Goldingay makes the point that, for a later audience, when the Amorites and the Canaanites were no more, this would teach the Jewish people to live at peace with their neighbours.[4]

## Law for living in the land

Chapters 4 and 5 bring us back to the ten commandments, a repeat of Exodus 20:1–17, with a long introduction underlining three unique things about Israel's God:

- He is close at hand (but not to be seen)
- He tolerates no rivals (and will stop at nothing to remove idol-worship)
- He keeps covenant with his people (because he is merciful).

Chapters 6–8 connect obedience to God's law with occupation of the good land made ready for the people of Israel. Most English versions say in 7:2, that God commands Israel to destroy the Canaanites, which western readers find difficult, if not outrageous. Three considerations cast some light on this:

1. In Abraham's time, the Canaanites were respected local inhabitants. By the time Israel comes to occupy the land, they have reverted to homosexual rape and child sacrifice. In the words of John Goldingay, "God has been giving them rope for centuries, and they have hanged themselves."[5]
2. There is no suggestion that what the Israelites were told to do should apply to other nations.
3. The purpose of Scripture is to form attitudes, for good and against evil. When Jesus said it was better to lose an eye than look at a woman with lust, he was not literally telling people to pluck out their eyes. While in these early days the Jewish people

were certainly fighting for land, later many did not take these instructions literally, and most thought that only the Messiah should take up arms to bring world peace.

"Do you really think the people of Israel really killed all the Canaanites?" asked Jean.

"Well, that passage in chapter 7 goes on to say 'don't intermarry with them', and since we discover later on that the Canaanites were not in fact destroyed, the word in its context may mean 'regard them as totally off-limits'. In any case, things are not always as they seem. For example, in 13:5 Moses calls for false prophets to be executed, but later Israel did not take this literally. They saw it as a call for right attitudes, a call to take holiness seriously. The people of God were to be different from the surrounding nations."

Different—but in what way? Difference is such a weasel word, as this poem suggests in a modern context:

### Learning to Differentiate

*"Vive la difference!"*
Oh what a difference
context and correctness
make to ancient custom.
These schools with
toilets strictly unisex,
strictly built to tolerate
transgender choice,
they end up blurring
sexual difference,
though who we are
is certainly not based
upon our sexuality,
but on that old
forgotten phrase,
"made in God's image".

## The heart of it

A central short passage is the *shema* ("Hear, O Israel") of 6:4–9, which includes the command to "love the Lord your God with all your heart and with all your soul and with all your might", the word "heart" in Hebrew indicating the bodily centre of what today we call "mind" and "will".

"That's obviously where Jesus got his answer to the Pharisee," said Jean, again surprising me by what she already knew about the Bible.

"Yes, and a neat way to focus on the heart of true religion," I said to her, aware how much damage religious passions cause when they run riot.

### Praying Passion (Deuteronomy 6:4–6)

Flush out the wax
with the oil of your Spirit.
Rush in the word
that will sweeten my soul
and make my heart leap
with the mind-lifting sweep
of your love for the world.

Leave out the dust
that has clouded my senses.
Weave in the duty
~~of hearing your teaching,~~
of reading and praying
with passion, obeying
your will for the world.

Rake out the ashes
of failure and faithlessness.
Take in the sparks
of my hopes and my dreams,
make my deepest desire
a slow-burning fire
that will light up the world.

"Do religious people really light up the world?" Probably a rhetorical question from Jean, but I answered it.

"Some do. And later on the prophet Isaiah said that God's servant would be 'a light for the nations'. Many Jews understand that reference to 'servant' as meaning the people of Israel."

"Why did God choose that people anyway?"

"A modern verse line goes: 'How odd of God to choose the Jews.'"

"Yes, I've heard that," said Jean. "And I know the second line, 'But not so odd as those who choose a Jewish God, and spurn the Jews.'"

The mystery of election, God choosing, is referred to in 7:7, where the Jews were chosen in spite of being "the fewest of all peoples". God shows his covenant love "to a thousand generations" (7:9). This small nation will possess a land which is fertile, where they can mine iron and copper (8:7–9). But they must continue to live, not by bread alone, "but by every word that comes from the mouth of the Lord" (8:3).

# Hard choice

### Testing, Testing (Deuteronomy, especially 8:2–10)

This poem's a sestina, somewhat off
the wall, a pilgrimage through desert
country with no money in the bank.
You're tested on this trip, because the simple
fact that faces you is this: the grave
you dug your friend last night may be *your* end

Do I exaggerate? Not much: the end
God has in mind is forty long years off,
which signifies "the cradle to the grave".
The journey is a challenge—yet the desert
rain will flush out tiny flowers, simple
reds and blues to flash out of a sandbank.

You fear that Moses is a mountebank,
an own agenda man, who in the end
will be exposed. You long for Egypt, simple
days and warmer nights. You had it off
the shelf back there, no gathering tasteless desert
food, none of this oversight so grave

and godly, all because God did engrave
those ten commands into a databank
of stone—although you soon were to desert
those rules, and party; Moses put an end
to that, and all; no wonder, it was off
the scale—an orgy, not so pure and simple.

Finally you twigged. With God, life's simple,
straight and satisfying. Yes, the grave
will come, one day they'll say *you'll shuffle off*
*this mortal coil*, and then they'll freeze your bank
account; but someone else will say, *your end*
*is your beginning*, even in the desert.

All of this is not your own desert
– as if! It seems that God with his own simple
wisdom has embraced you, just to upend
how we do religious stuff, engrave
his word upon your heart, and even bank
his project hopes on you to pull it off.

To brave the desert risks an early grave –
but you can bank on God. Just keep life simple:
in the end, you will be better off.

"Shakespeare and T. S. Eliot were both trying to make sense of the human journey, in their different ways," said Jean.

And that is what the final editor of Deuteronomy must have been trying to do—to take hold of the journey from Egypt to the promised land, and offer it to his own generation as a model of how we learn to obey God. And being Hebrew language, this chapter 8 is full of verbs which resonate with anyone trying to discern what God is up to in human life: God bringing us into a good place, resources flowing into our lives or welling up deep inside us, stuff to be mined through hard work, all in the context of "remember the Lord your God" (8:18).

Several times the text underlines that the land will be a gift, not a right, and that Israel herself may forfeit the land if she disobeys God, just as the other wicked nations are going to forfeit the land. The people may be chosen, but they are chosen to model the meaning of grace, and the generosity of God, not because they deserve God's blessing (chapter 9).

## Law as a fence for the poor

Chapter 10 refers to Moses carving the tablets a second time, and celebrates aspects of the law that we easily overlook:

- Law is for our good (verse 13)
- Law must be taken into the heart (verse 16)
- Law commands love, even of strangers (verse 19)
- Law is from a God who has done great things for his people (verses 21–22).

Deuteronomy celebrates law, although (as the poem hints) that law will need to be written on the human heart before it is fully effective. Nevertheless law teaches us how to live, and good laws hold a society together.

In ancient times, the ode celebrated great things and greater kings, but more recent poets have used its reverent and reflective spirit to reference a wide range of objects and occasions. The next poem commends law which protects the innocent and the vulnerable, and questions the principle of usury—an issue which at one time or other has exercised all three major monotheistic religions.

## Ode to Law

Who wants to laud what Paul has damned
with faint praise ("Good, but just a gaoler")?[6]
Crude words, if used about a book jammed

hard and fast and sharp against the failure
of the kings of Israel, yet deftly slipping
into fifth place in the Torah trailer

for the rest of Scripture—sermons stripping
away cantankerous rant from East and West
so near the tipping point, and clipping

cant which can't see clear the blest
and curst things: "Shed no innocent blood,
protect the foreigner, charge no interest."

Good law's a fence, defence against a flood
of evil enterprise, and all lies rammed
so rudely down the throat of man and God.

"I thought that the Jewish people were destined to become money-lenders, at least in many people's minds," said Jean, who had already done a rapid read of Deuteronomy, and had spotted 15:6.

"Well, it suited medieval times, when Europe needed capital but Christians were not supposed to charge interest. Jews were forbidden to charge interest to fellow-Jews—that's clear from Exodus 22:25—but they could to foreigners. And now that Muslim countries are growing their economies, it's an issue for them too."

"How do you mean?"

"Well, so-called Islamic banks are on the increase. But most of them practise what they call *murabahah*, which is just an alternative way of charging interest. Purists say that is wrong, that the right way is *musharakah*, in which the bank takes part-ownership and shares the risk of profit or loss."

We decided to get back to Deuteronomy. The importance of the law is rehearsed again and again, as a protection for people and land. In 11:18–20 it becomes literally a fence for families, and even today you will find a little law scroll on the wall outside hotel rooms in Jerusalem.

In chapter 12, all pagan shrines are to be demolished, and this clearly has a later situation in view (12:2). By contrast, the Israelites are to worship at one central place; for later readers, obviously Jerusalem;[7] and in Josiah's time Judah was a small area where this made sense. In later centuries, time and again a ruler would use this teaching to justify centralising religious power; one thinks of the way the Roman practice of Christianity outlawed Celtic practices.[8] And there has been endless debate about whether and how different Christian churches could or should unite.

## Democratic origins

In thirteenth-century England, Archbishop Stephen Langton was influenced by his reading of Deuteronomy, and its teaching that law must favour neither rich nor poor. He drafted the famous *Magna Carta*, the "Great Charter". This poem was written to mark the 800th anniversary of its acceptance by King John.

### Magna Carta

> Today the English must remember
> what Lord Denning once described
> as all time great: a document
> that first laid claim to human rights.
> Eleven times my living span
> is serious ageing in reverse,
> and all for what? A Baron's Charter
> signed and spun as Magna Carta.

Bishop Langton wrote it, called
the council that first backed it.
Pope annulled it, king reduced it,
but it entered statute law.
Some will praise it, like Obama
(even if he worked outside it),
some dismiss it, as that tartar
Cromwell called it Magna Farta.

Robert Bruce complained to Edward
that he disobeyed and dodged what
Langton saw, and kept in mind: that
king and commoner keep the same
clear Deuteronomic obligation.
When the chips are on the table,
we need equal law, not art, a
better deal than Magna Carta.

Here in Scotland, we the people
need a written constitution
and much more. Where will we find
a proper ground for liberties, that's
real, respected, democratic?
The British State is slow to start a
move like this, but do take heart: a
long time's passed since Magna Carta.

Jean said she thought ideas about democracy were modern ideas from
"The Enlightenment". I confess I enjoyed enlightening her. "They really
came from the Old Testament, which at first sight is about theocracy, rule
by God. And it wasn't just bishops who got the message, or Alexander
Melville in Scotland calling James VI 'God's sillie vassal'—it was the
Puritans who really developed ideas about democracy in radical ways,
people like John Milton or John Lilburne; John Locke picked up his 'all
men born free and equal' from them."

## Animals, tithes, debt

The rules about clean and unclean foods are probably more about keeping Israel distinct from the other nations than about hygiene, but one verse may have special importance (14:21): "You shall not boil a kid in its mother's milk". Bible followers have been pilloried for mistreating animals and the planet in general, on the basis of Genesis 1:28, to "have dominion over". However the context of Genesis, and this verse in Deuteronomy, make clear that "dominion" means "responsible stewardship", and puts a sharp question to such practices as factory farming.

It is not to our credit that human concern for animals has so often been left to a minority, even if it includes film stars as this poem recalls:

### The Ballad of Brigitte Bardot

Trust a cat to look after itself
and its litter,
predictably perch on the lap
of its sitter,
no hint of the fallout and angst
from the quarrels
of life spent on film, but a rest
from the laurels
of fame, and a paw you can hold
without fear
it will scratch you or fight you in court.
Your career
brought you one hundred lovers,
four husbands,
but led to depression and worse,
so your hands
turned to stroking a posse of cats
and your nights
to embracing and stoking a passion
for animal rights.

Good preaching takes what is written in the Bible and applies it to contemporary life. We see this already happening in chapter 14, with the regulations about tithes, and in chapter 15, where the original "jubilee" for land is applied to wealth and debt. Moses prophesies that his people will one day be lenders to the nations, not borrowers (verse 6, as Jean had spotted). In the Middle Ages, Jewish merchants became great lenders, as usury (charging interest) was forbidden by the Christian Church.

"So that is why Shakespeare wrote *The Merchant of Venice!*" said Jean.

"Well, like all writers I guess he poked around in a lot of contemporary backyards. Although Jewish texts of the period promoted fair practice, prejudice grew against people like Shylock."

Jewish commentators distinguished between lending for development and creativity, which could charge interest, and lending to help the needy, which should be interest-free, on the basis of the difference between lending to foreigners and to fellow-Jews in chapter 15 (and also 23:19–20).

There is also a new text, which Jesus was to quote,[9] recognising that poverty as such would never be eradicated (15:11), and so in parallel the command to be generous to the poor would last for ever. These texts indicate that such generosity must be shown both personally and politically. Tolstoy wrote sarcastically of the landed classes who felt sorry for the poor, would give them food and point out to them the beauties of the landscape—people who would do everything except get off their backs. This short piece of verse recalls Tolstoy's words.

### After Tolstoy (Deuteronomy 15:7–11)

Get off my back,
give me some air,
at least a breath
to show you care;
I'm not from Mars,
I'm human, see,
and what is more
you'll die like me.

In all this, Deuteronomy does not take for granted that selling your labour is the norm—the norm is a family working together on the land. Even someone who wants to stay a servant works within that context.[10] We assume today that such an approach is outdated—but we desperately need new economic models to replace or amend the capitalism which is clearly not managing to address the question of poverty in the world, and instead adds each year to the gap between rich and poor.

## Pilgrims and prophets

The next chapter reviews the three great festivals (Passover, Harvest, Tabernacles) which required pilgrimage to the one central place of worship, bringing an offering. For the followers of Judaism, Jerusalem is still the place of pilgrimage, but the Feast of Tabernacles was later associated with the coming of the nations to join Israel in worship.[11]

"Do you know that I once climbed Mount Sinai?" I said to Jean. We had decided to go for a walk along the Water of Leith, and share a bit more of our own journeys.

"What was it like?" asked Jean.

"Not at all what I expected. There is a monastery there, and Margaret and I were staying in the guest house outside because women were not allowed in the monastery itself. We had to get up in the middle of the night, make our way to the camel station and ride up the mountain on camels."

"Wasn't it too steep for a camel?"

"Only at the top, where there was a very long flight of steps. But what really took me by surprise was the Bedouin café on top. And a crowd of Africans. When I enquired whether this was a special pilgrimage, a Nigerian told me that they went up every year!"

Pilgrimage is a multi-national activity. This poem was written in memory of Andrew Patterson, an indefatigable pilgrim, biker, expert guide to many pilgrim routes such as the Camino de Santiago. When his first wife died, Andrew took time out to live and journey on a canal boat.

## An Honest Pilgrimage

No need for Chaucer to unleash his scrutiny
of pilgrim motives; no necessity for Bunyan
following up his progress to a city;
here we find a plain and honest man
whom God has taken, dusted down and led
to serve his fellows as a councillor
with honest counsel; humble teacher, well read,
pilgrim biker, then an all-round minister
who earned and learned this trusted role as fighter
for the underdog, a listener, lover
caring to the bitter end, a writer
on the pilgrim way himself—a brother.

So, that slow canal boat journey, thinning
into tunnel dark, is over: now a new beginning.

Priests generally support established authority, prophets challenge it. Chapter 17 warns that a king must not acquire many horses and many wives (verses 14–17), likely to be a later reference to Solomon. Rather, a sovereign should have a copy of the law to read and practise, which among other things means that such a leader must not be exalted above other members of the community.

"Sounds like having a bicycle monarchy," was Jean's comment.

"That's why Queen Elizabeth II was presented with a copy of the Bible at her coronation. It was styled 'the royal law.'"

By priests, by prophets, and by the law is God's mind and purpose to be found. Sandwiched between text about priests and prophets in chapter 18 is a condemnation of sorcery and what today is called spiritualism. Along with child sacrifice, such practices are abhorrent, and lead to people being driven out of their land.

While prophecy is generally regarded as "forth-telling" rather than "foretelling", the prophet is also a "seer", one who sees what God is up to, and what will happen in the future if people do not heed what is being said. So a prophet may be tested by whether what is said comes true or not

(18:22). The passage saying that God will raise up a prophet like Moses "from among your own people" (18:15) was later applied by Stephen to the Messiah that Jewish people rejected (Acts 7:37).

## Protection

Priests and prophets will, in different ways, protect God's people, but there is a specific provision in chapter 19 for cities of refuge, which restates the rules of Numbers 35. Law should protect as well as accuse, and a single witness is not enough for a conviction (19:15).

Reference to a law court switched Jean's mind to her brother, and her attempt to make contact with him. "I got no reply from the Home," she said, "so I rang them up. They told me Jim was now in the Royal, and not very well. I'm going through this week to see him."

I recognised that Jean was in the middle of her own battle of conscience, and trying to escape from the shame which had clouded her relationship with her half-brother. This time I thought I might be able to draw a lesson from Deuteronomy without her thinking I was preaching at her.

"No fight is easy, whether you're in the Armed Services or in your own personal battle. At the start of chapter 20, a priest comes forward to encourage the army, and says, 'Listen, today you are going into battle. Do not lose courage. The Lord your God is going with you, and he will give you victory.' I think that also applies to our own battles."

There are rules of warfare, designed to protect—for example, to release from fighting a man who has just got engaged. It is the priest, not the general, who decides who should fight and who should not. Terms of peace should be offered before battle, and fruit trees should be spared (chapter 20).

## Trees (Deuteronomy 20:19–20)

Carbon-capturing crown of plant life,
standing glory of protected parkland,
arboretum focus, forest resident,
every woodsman's wonder,
lungs of a well-built town.

Vulnerable to every planning quirk,
mono-cultured for a faster buck,
bonsaied for the indoor experience,
chain-sawn while the neighbours
watch, and feel the pain.

Without that line in Deuteronomy,
who knows? Zacchaeus and his like
might still be waiting, grounded,
without a chance to rise above
the crowd, and meet their Master.

The commands in Deuteronomy even touch on birds' nests as well as trees. To appreciate these rules, and those found in the following chapters, it is wise to recognise that Deuteronomy is realistic rather than idealistic. Larger issues such as war, murder, polygamy and divorce were facts of life. The text recognises this and seeks to regulate them. For those who like connections, Calvin got the Council of Geneva to introduce building safety regulations on the basis of 22:8.

Some of the laws concern sexual relations, what boundaries to set, and what to do when sex goes wrong (22:13–30). Those who can remember the 1950s in Britain and America will feel in home country here, those who only know the "permissive society" may find it quaint. Most Jews, Christians and Muslims share the belief that sex is not a casual act but belongs within marriage, and there is no good evidence that other approaches have made life safer or better for women and girls.

Some years ago the Church of Scotland debated whether a man who had killed his mother could later, if he showed repentance, become a minister. Sometimes the Bible can be used to support two different positions (which is, of course, why debates can be so difficult). For example, 23:3 bans Ammonites and Moabites from the assembly of the Lord—yet Ruth was a Moabite and regarded as a heroine![12]

## Economics and ethics

Certain commands commend what John Goldingay calls "sacred inefficiency".[13] The poor should be allowed to benefit from a farmer not maximising his yield (23:24–25, 24:19–21).

"That's all very well with small farms and peasants," said Jean, "But it wouldn't work with combine harvesters and big fields—and people living in cities."

"The Bible is not a textbook on economics or science; it isn't even a textbook on ethics. Textbooks have to be written again and again for every generation and every culture. But it does tell us how God sees things, and how we might choose to see one another."

"Both Karl Marx and Margaret Thatcher quoted the Bible. It's easy to find a text to suit your own purposes."

"Yes, in Martin Luther's words it's easy for the Bible to become 'a nose of wax', which can be pulled any way you like."

"So capitalists point out that, in the parable of the ten talents in the New Testament, Jesus tells the one-talent man who buried his money in the ground that he should have taken it to the bankers to get some interest. And socialists cite the first Christians who shared their property so that each person could get what they needed."

Jean was a living reminder of how, until about 1970, everyone knew quite a lot of the Bible. I had to think carefully about my reply.

"In the New Testament, God's people are individuals called to become small groups of people—'church'—who would live in the middle of a hostile society, making their own relationships honest and caring. In the Old Testament, we see what is supposed to happen when a whole nation is called to live as God's people. There will be lessons we can pick up from both. That's the challenge to Jews and Christians, to anyone who takes the Bible seriously as God's word."[14]

Jean was remembering her opportunities to teach philosophy in school. "Back in eighteenth-century Scotland, philosophy wasn't the narrow business it has become in universities today. Science was known as 'natural philosophy', and economics was known as 'political economy'."

"And Adam Smith, the so-called 'father of free enterprise', didn't just write *The Wealth of Nations*—before that he wrote *The Theory of Moral Sentiments*! He recognised that government had a role to ensure that markets were fair as well as free. There is a statue to him in Edinburgh's High Street, and it gave me an idea for this poem."

### Adam Smith

He thought well. He meant well. He lived well.
He deserves this statue by the City Chambers
to the author of *The Wealth of Nations*.

Is he not the father of free enterprise?
He has earned this jacket with eleven buttons,
this cloak, this curled wig, this reputation.

Now his eyes and lips are bronze, to match
the hearts of those who cherry-pick his writings,
leaving out his checks and balances to power.

The way Deuteronomy links ethics to public life is to attach commands to the instruction, "Remember that you were a slave in the land of Egypt". It is when people accept their common humanity, and recognise how easily it is abused, that a society is likely to have laws and practices which care for the poor. One text in particular (26:5) became like a motto for Israel: "A wandering Aramean was my ancestor . . ." Abraham is the great ancestor of the Jewish people; although his time in Egypt did him little credit (Genesis 12:10–20), it became part of the great story which is celebrated in 26:5-9, and used as part of the liturgy at harvest festivals.

## Remembering the journey

When the journey is complete, on the day the people cross over the Jordan into the promised land, they are to set up plastered stones with the law written upon them, on Mount Ebal. This hill is on the northern side, with Mount Gerizim on the southern side of the valley in which Nablus today is located, on the West Bank. Six tribes will stand on Mount Gerizim for the blessing of the people, six tribes on Mount Ebal for the curse. Blessings and curses are outlined in chapters 27 and 28.

The warnings against disobedience include a fairly detailed description of the hardships that would overtake Israel through the Babylonian siege and exile, another sign of how this material was edited later on during the exile, and a reminder to every generation that what God says should be applied afresh in new contexts.

"These texts are as explicit as some modern writing," said Jean. "Mothers eating their own children during a siege, for example—and I spotted one reference to eating the afterbirth as well (28:57). I was reading Gavin Francis' book *Adventures in Human Being*, all about our amazing bodies, and there is a whole chapter on afterbirth.[15] Bet you haven't got a poem about that!"

"You enjoy these digressions—I expect you call it lateral thinking. That's one of the nice things about poetry, it does let you wander into odd corners of life—but I will need to make a poem that is appropriate for the context, and not just an indulgence."

That was more of a challenge. Here is the result:

### After Birth, the Curse (Deuteronomy 28:57)

Eat it, bury it under a tree;
Burn it, float it out to sea;
how afterbirth is given honour
in so many different cultures,
as the strong, so long connection
tying foetal child to mother.

But here, consuming a placenta,
Israel siege-starved, meant a
curse, confirming something
worse than cannibal practice,
swallowing all their future
life, hope and everything.

"Maybe I shouldn't have asked you," said Jean.

"It is a gloomy poem," I admitted, "and I've never heard a sermon on that text. But it is part of human history. Remember Picasso and Guernica."

Deuteronomy 29:4 says that the people don't understand what they have experienced. So maybe that poem is not such a digression; we experience these extraordinary bodies of ours, and only a few experts really know what is going on. And our bodies politic go through extraordinary changes, and we depend on a few prophetic figures to tell us what is really going on. That is what Deuteronomy was doing for Israel; after all, Moses was called a prophet, and just as key thinkers today need to be published in some form of media, so Moses needed to be published by scribes later on.

When the Israelites reached the land of Moab, the covenant was renewed. Again this meant remembering the journey. Chapter 29 ends with a verse which appears suddenly out of context, but is typical of the balance shown in many of the Deuteronomic commands. What is secret belongs to God, what is revealed belongs to us and our children. Why? So that we may do what God tells us (29:29).

In chapter 30, there is a promise of return from exile (verse 4), and a promise that God will "circumcise the heart", language which connects with the prophets Jeremiah and Ezekiel. As for the commands, they are right before the people, "in your mouth and in your heart" (30:14).[16] Deuteronomy sets out what God requires, then challenges people to choose the right way, and in so doing to choose life, not death.[17] The whole law is to be read aloud every seventh year (31:9–11).

## A great view

Moses is now near the end of his life. He is told to commission Joshua as his successor, and the Lord again appears in a pillar of cloud, as on the journey out of Egypt (31:15). The book closes with "the song of Moses", the great law-giver, which is a further rehearsal of the story of the journey and its relevance to Israel—"no trifling matter, but rather your very life" (32:47). In the final chapter Moses looks over the promised land of Canaan before he dies.

"I see Moses described God as a father to Israel in that song."

I sensed there might be a question behind this. "Yes, and it's quite a tender expression."

"Is God ever described as a mother?"

"Not in so many words. But later in the Bible God is described like a mother with a nursing child."[18]

In 32:11 the Lord is compared to an eagle teaching its young to fly. The Hebrew word does not specify gender, though it is sometimes translated as a mother eagle; in fact, eagles pair for life and both parents teach their offspring to fly. The approach the Bible takes in unequal societies is generally to accept current practice but to require care and consideration within that; this will in turn fuel wider change later on—as eventually happened both with patriarchy and with slavery.

At the top of Mount Nebo (now a built-over area in Jordan) is a sculpture showing a snake on a pole, from the story in Numbers 21:4–9 (referred to later on in John 3:14). While Moses was the one who made a bronze snake for those bitten (as a result of their grumbling) to look at and be healed, this sculpture was put up at the point where Moses was allowed to look over Canaan from Mount Nebo, but not enter (as a result, ironically, of his own shortcoming). The next poem was written watching two tourists approach the sculpture, one flippant, the other humble.

### Two Tourists (Deuteronomy 32:48–51)

Sculpted for tourists: just too easy a reminder of a
life and death encounter in the Jordan desert;
serpentine symbol for good and for evil,
lifted high for healing and for hope;
do we stand and smile beside it,
or approach with bowed head,
uncertain where to place our feet,
remembering him whose body and soul
were torn and broken for our sin at Golgotha?
Lord, scalp my pride, and sculpt my raw material.

In ancient literature the snake is a symbol for healing, as in the context of the Hippocratic oath, but also a symbol of temptation and wickedness (as in Genesis 3). This double meaning attaches itself to many ideas in the Bible; the law is good, but shows up our sin; humankind is made in the image of God, but that image is flawed; the love of God is pure and good, attracting us wonderfully—yet the same love judges us when we ignore it.

After a last blessing of the tribes in chapter 33, at the end of Deuteronomy Moses is celebrated as the greatest prophet in Israel (34:10–12). Both Moses and Abraham are great travellers for God: one stands for law, the other for promise, two ideas which shape character in different ways, and remain in dialogue throughout the Bible.

# Notes

1   See Gerhard Von Rad, *Deuteronomy* (SCM, 1966), p. 14.

2   The name actually comes from a mistranslation into Greek of "copy" in 17:18.

3   See Ian Cairns, *Word and Presence* (Eerdmans, 1992), p. 21.

4   John Goldingay, *Numbers and Deuteronomy for Everyone* (SPCK, 2010), pp. 102–103.

5   *Numbers and Deuteronomy for Everyone*, p. 118.

6   Galatians 3:23.

7   In 2 Chronicles 30 Hezekiah invites all those in Israel (the north) as well as Judah to come to Jerusalem to keep the Passover.

8   At the Synod of Whitby, AD 664.

9   Matthew 26:11, also in Mark's and John's Gospels.

10  *Numbers and Deuteronomy for Everyone*, p. 148.

11  From Zechariah 14:16.

12  But the debate continued: according to the Babylonian Talmud, Doeg the Edomite used David's descent from Ruth to argue against him being the true king (1 Samuel 22 illustrates his loyalty to King Saul).

13  *Numbers and Deuteronomy for Everyone*, p. 124.

14  Perhaps I should have pointed out that in the parable of the talents it is "the hard employer", not Jesus, who recommends seeking interest. Right up to 1500 the Christian Church followed the Old Testament in condemning interest—and maybe they had a point. See, for example, the discussion by Paul Mills and Michael Schluter in *After Capitalism: Rethinking Economic Relationships* (Jubilee Centre, 2012).

15  Gavin Francis, *Adventures in Human Being* (Wellcome, 2015).

16  Paul was to cite this in Romans 10:8.

17  Deuteronomy 30:15.

18  Isaiah 49:15.

CHAPTER 7

# Joshua

Military history is a popular genre; what makes the book of Joshua a challenge, in its context, is the on-going conflict over land in the Middle East, when at the same time all three monotheistic religions claim to be a religion of peace. Judaism, Christianity and Islam all revere documents which describe and advocate war in some circumstances, so the right interpretation of Old Testament, New Testament and the Qur'an is of crucial importance when the old twentieth-century view that "religion doesn't matter, it's just about politics" is so obviously wrong.

I was also aware that Jean was fighting her own battle—with herself, as she told me after she had managed to locate her brother Jim in ward 25 of Glasgow Royal Infirmary. "I didn't tell you everything about Jim and me when I was still a child," was all she said. "Seeing him now has brought a lot back."

We were about to start on Joshua. I was aware of the ambiguities of the book, revealed at the start when chapter 1 underlines the importance of reading God's law in public worship, while chapter 2 introduces a prostitute as heroine, a woman who lies brazenly about the spies staying in her house. In that, Rahab follows the example of two heroines of the book of Exodus—the midwives Shiphrah and Puah who lie to Pharaoh—reminding us that standing up to males who exercise authority badly is not unknown in the Bible.

Nevertheless the book also has a simple message, about courage, trusting a God who says he will be with you. I had already written a poem trying to reflect that simplicity, which I shared with Jean. She knew of course that Joshua was the same name as Jesus.

**Thinking of Joshua (Joshua 1:1–9)**

Apprentice, acolyte, warrior, scout,
trained for leadership from early on
by Moses: this Joshua/Jesus is all about
courage, faith, that resolve to carry on

obeying, the way God imagined things.
He needs every promise, all he can get
from a God who says he'll give wings
to his feet as he walks each day; yet

from Joshua to me is a long, long way
– like crossing the Jordan—Lord, show me
you're here right beside me, come what may;
lead me, follow me; after all, you know me.

# The River Jordan

"I feel like I'm on the wrong side of the Jordan," said Jean. "Or perhaps just wishing some river could wash away a lot of stuff downstream."

I listened to her for a while. Then we drifted back to Joshua, still camped on the wrong side of Jordan. The Jordan is for the most part a small, rather dirty river, which floods at harvest time (3:14).

## Jordan in Flood

Such a small river,
but when it floods
it carries memories like grey silt
and laps them at my feet.

I start, draw back,
look each way
searching for a brighter colour,
or even black and white.

Grey, eyeing me,
the known unknown,
or is it the unknown known
I have to rediscover?

The muck will touch me,
slither up my legs,
aim for my heart and lungs.
I freeze, horrified.

Then I see them:
the others, in the flood,
carrying their own box of memories.
I must get my feet wet.

"You don't usually do that in your poems," Jean pointed out.

"Do what?"

"Use allegory. As the slaves did when they wrote those spirituals."

"It's not fashionable to use the Bible that way nowadays, but a lot of people did in the past. The great example is seeing the River Jordan as the river to cross when you die, but I think it's a good symbol for anything that threatens you—whether it is our past or our future. Yet I must admit I never thought about the ark carried by the priests as a box of memories till I wrote that poem."

The spies have done their job, and have agreed that Rahab and her family will be spared when the Israelites take her city. Rahab's narrative in chapter 2 implies that the story of Exodus is well known, and that there is already a "fifth column" within Jericho (as there turned out to be with the Gibeonites in chapter 9). But before we reach the battle of Jericho in chapter 6, other things have to happen.

## Old stones

We were in the St Giles' café when Jean mentioned a book of poems she had just bought, called *Building Jerusalem*.[1]

"Lovely poetry," she said, "but quite depressing. All about these English churches which are either already ruined or in terminal decline. People who wanted to pass on their faith—and look what has happened."

"At least the stones are still there. We'll still be able to read them when a generation of digital files becomes unreadable. Come to think of it, that's exactly what Joshua did when they crossed the Jordan—twelve stones in the middle when it was dry, and twelve stones at their camp site to be a memorial for generations to come."

## Where are the Stones? (Joshua 4:19–24)

Faith has skipped a generation.
Grandparents try to compensate,
a little desperate, perhaps too late,
but trying, guilt-struck, caring,
mixed up as our world to date.

They wish church stones would speak
a little louder, as stained glass
pictures used to. In this new elastic
culture, Facebook, virtual games
and texting mould our plastic

brains,[2] and short term thinking
moves our mental traffic codes
from right to left-brain modes
of practice. Gather living stones,
with faithful story in their lodes.

"Do you know Iain McGilchrist's great book?"[3] Jean asked. "About the left and right brain, and how these different ways of thinking have shaped the history of the western world?"

"A most unusual fellow. Not many Oxford lecturers in English become psychiatrists! I love books which bring together different areas of knowledge to make sense of the world."

# Holy war

By this time I was thinking more than Jean was about the wider implications of Joshua, and its militaristic tone. Can war ever be holy? John Goldingay[4] points out that it is only the delicate and affluent West which struggles with this—other eras, and the New Testament itself, have no issues with the conquest of Canaan; Israel is simply the agent of God's judgement on people for their wrongdoing. At the same time, the Bible gives us no precedent for this ever being repeated: the early Boers who identified their Trek with the journey of the children of Israel, thinking this gave them biblical warrant to exterminate the Xhosa (identified with the Amalekites, as we saw in Numbers), were totally out of order.

"Did you know that the main builder of the State of Israel, David Ben-Gurion, held Bible studies every two weeks to encourage a sense of Jewish identity?" said Jean one day, out of the blue.

"But Ben-Gurion did not believe in God!"

"True. But the Bible was the most important book in his life, and within that the book of Joshua."[5]

"The book of Joshua is not quite what it seems, though—I have a poem about this."

After the pause for circumcision in chapter 5, Joshua has a strange encounter with an angel (6:13–15), which hints that God has more to do than take sides in a human battle. This poem, written in perhaps less than heroic couplets, raises these wider questions.

### Boots and Brains

Construction manual for the Israeli settler
who'd like to follow Joshua to the letter,

write history as it ought to be, work around
a six-day clock to put facts on the ground?

Arab Christians will not read a book like that:
homes do not change hands by God's *fiat*.

*Tout commence en mystique, et finit en politique*[6]
– some truth in that, but still *assez cynique*.

Lawyers go for the jugular: Martian war-gods,
or just Barthian thought-pods? Logic prods

the sceptic into such an alien choice
of spiritual or real: let's give the text its voice

and marvel at this story-line of Jericho
and Jordan, Gilgal, Hebron and Shiloh.

Some find a gem or two of spiritual gold,
unlike (of course) how Achan's tale was told,

but best to read unstressed by critics' press
of options, hear God's army general address

the matter with a soul and body swerve
and say, sword drawn, that Joshua has a nerve

to claim that God takes sides in human battles.
Take off your boots, for here the matter settles.

"Barthian thought-pods?" said Jean. "And you pride yourself on avoiding jargon?"

"I'm sorry. I do need to explain that reference. The theologian Karl Barth cited Joshua 1:1–11 in one of his books[7] and wrote that the occupation of Canaan must be understood as 'supremely active acceptance'. He solved the problem by saying that it's just an allegory."

"That would get him off the hook. Otherwise he would have had to support the State of Israel, wouldn't he?"

"It's not as simple as that. But many people do see the establishment of the Israeli State as an act of divine providence, following the holocaust."

"Some no doubt see it as a fulfilment of the promise made to Abraham."

"And others feel the balance of power in the Middle East has shifted so much that the Israeli State has become an oppressor as was the case in *apartheid* South Africa."

We left it there. Both of us realised that the problems of the Middle East had no simple human solution.

I referred to Achan in that poem. That story is in chapter 7, following the story of the famous battle; it tells how one man took some gold from the enemy and hid it in his tent; when Israel lost the next battle, God told Joshua there was a moral issue; Achan was picked out by lot, and stoned to death. The lesson here, repeated time and again throughout the Old Testament, is that God is not racist—when the people of God sin, they are held to account just like anyone else (perhaps more so).

People have speculated how the Jericho "walls came a-tumblin' down". As usual, the account just says what happened. It is the ritual that is emphasised: the daily early morning march round the city with trumpets sounding, and on the seventh day doing this seven times, with that final shout, often taken to be a short version of the holy name of God, "Yah". Rahab and her family, as we would hope, were rescued.

The strange incident of the angel is placed just before the battle of Jericho, perhaps to emphasise that this is indeed "holy" war (and therefore, perhaps, never to be repeated).

## The conquest of the land

One of the striking things about Joshua is that chapters 8–12, especially 11:16, 11:23 and 12:7–24, present Joshua capturing the whole land; chapter 13 indicates that there is still much land to be taken; while in 21:43–45 the job is finished—which, if the book of Judges is to be believed, is far from being the case.

From a strictly historical point of view, it is clear that the conquest was gradual. Deuteronomy 7:22 indicates that had the conquest happened too quickly, the land would be overrun by wild animals, while the books that follow Joshua present Israel's struggle with the Philistines and other local peoples, up to the reign of King David.

The interest of those who compiled the Old Testament books is theological. This does not mean that they simply invented what they record, but it does mean that they selected and shaped their material to teach Israel what it meant to be the people of God.

"So why these two rather different views of the conquest of Canaan?" asked Jean.

"Maybe it's to teach us about the 'now' and 'not yet'. What God does is complete and perfect, yet when God is dealing with ordinary and fallible human beings it can take a long time to work through. For example, God takes his people out of Egypt, but it takes a long time to get Egypt out of the people. God really does take his people into a promised land, but it takes a long time for them to become the sort of people who can look after that land properly. And, of course, each leader dies without seeing that vision fulfilled."

"That makes the Old Testament a story of failure, doesn't it?"

"Depends how you look at it. Think of our own lives. We achieve a few things, fail in others, then grow old and die. It all depends what lies in front of us—whether there is a 'not yet'."

Instead of writing a poem, my mind went to an old hymn which links two ideas—the journey of faith and the fight of faith. While the writer was no doubt thinking of his journey as an escape from a bad "now" to a better heavenly home, his words inspired many others to fight against evils like slavery, and those same people would have seen Joshua's clearance of the Canaanites as their own call to clear social and industrial evils from their own land in the nineteenth century.

> "For ever with the Lord!" Amen, so let it be!
> Life from the dead is in that word, 'tis immortality.
> Here, in the body pent, absent from him I roam,
> Yet nightly pitch my moving tent a day's march nearer home.
>
> "For ever with the Lord!" Father, if 'tis thy will
> The promise of that faithful word e'en here to me fulfil.
> Be thou at my right hand, then I can never fail;
> Uphold thou me, and I shall stand; fight, and I must prevail.
>
> So, when my latest breath shall rend the veil in twain,
> By death I shall escape from death and life eternal gain.
> That resurrection word, that shout of victory;
> Once more, "For ever with the Lord!" Amen, so let it be![8]

Coming back to Joshua, I added rather frankly that the story of the Old Testament was largely the tale of how the Israelites became as bad as or worse than the nations they replaced, until they in turn had to be taken into exile.

"That's pretty grim, isn't it?"

"It's realistic. The Bible is there to help us relate to life as it really is. There is plenty about getting beyond the grit and the grime, but God works through just those things."

"It's still tough on the Canaanites, being driven out of their land just because God was doing an experiment with the Hebrews. You did say you'd come back to that when we got to Joshua."

While Jericho was an important battle, the heart of the book of Joshua is the battle with the various Amorite kings. In a way it was a defensive battle, because the Amorites were threatening to attack Gibeon, which had made peace with Israel (chapter 9). While Joshua's tactics were superior, a feature of the battle was the hailstones which fell and are said to have killed more Amorites than did the swords of the Israelites. To make clear that it was God who gave the victory, the (unknown) *Book of Jashar* recorded the tale of a unique long day which gave Joshua extra time to win the battle.

## The power of land

In Abraham's day, the Canaanites were often his friends. But Genesis 15:16 suggests that at some later time "the sin of the Amorites" became so bad that they deserved to be driven out of the land. According to Deuteronomy 12:31 it included child sacrifice. The conquest is therefore presented as a moral act of God's judgement. However, much later on, 2 Kings 21:11 tells us that King Manasseh of Israel was even more wicked than the Amorites, and Jeremiah 25:11 says that the Israelites in turn would be driven out of the land—for the sake of the land itself. Leviticus 18:25 warns that the land vomits out such people!

"Land is not just a 'natural resource'," I reflected, "it has its own ways, perhaps even its own standards."

"Do you know what MacDiarmid wrote about the land of his boyhood?" asked Jean.

"Tell me," I said.

"He wrote: 'Scotland is not generally regarded as a land flowing with milk and honey. Nevertheless . . . it certainly did in my boyhood, with a bountifulness so inexhaustible that it has supplied all my poetry . . . with a teeming gratitude of reminiscence."[9]

"'River Jordan is deep and wide, milk and honey on the other side.' Funny how that kind of language rubbed off on believer and atheist alike. But not in poetry today. Here is a villanelle I have just written about land."

### Resolution

Write up the loveliness of all these lands
that nestle between oceans, snug in coastlines.
Strike down the wickedness of human hands

that fix the rents sky high, pollute the sands
with plastic bags, with chemicals, and mines.
Write up the loveliness of all these lands:

Proclaim the flowers, trumpeting their brands
of flame, red roses sent as Valentines.
Strike down the wickedness of human hands:

Divert the fearsome tramp of fighting bands
of mercenaries, tangle them in vines.
Write up the loveliness of all these lands,

make sure that every person understands
how they may tease the word to read "love lines".
Strike down the wickedness of human hands?

> Well, that will take a God whose heart expands
> to heal the heartless, hug the Frankensteins.
> Write up the loveliness of all these lands;
> strike down the wickedness of human hands.

"I struggled with a title for that poem," I said.

"I can see it's about the need to look after land, and the cost of doing that. And that takes resolution. So the title works."

"Sure. And the Israelites did need plenty of resolve. But I wondered about 'Janus' because 'tease out' is so different from 'strike down.'"

"Janus? That old god with two heads?"

"I know it doesn't really work. It was the people who kept looking two ways."

The Song of Moses back in Deuteronomy 32 recognised that Israel would look back to Egypt as well as forward to the land of promise. It's human nature. The books that follow Joshua would show this all too clearly. But the first twelve chapters of Joshua are largely about victory, and relate to the territory of Benjamin and the worship centre of Gilgal.[10] Later on (18:1) the holy tent was set up at Shiloh.

## More about land

While chapters 13 onwards may appear less interesting, the allotment of land to the different tribes is important, first because it is a fulfilment of God's promise and command (21:43–45), and second because in the Old Testament, something as material as land is a spiritual matter. Land ownership and use today is still a matter of controversy.

"Did you know that 8% of Scotland is owned by just sixteen people, and 50% by fewer than a thousand?" said Jean, obviously wanting to make connections.

"It's not easy to find out these things. Where did you get that from?"

"Andy Wightman's book."[11]

Wightman helped the Green Party to develop their policy of land value taxation. Not quite as radical as the Jubilee Principle of Leviticus 25, but in its way trying to do what exercises Joshua in these chapters, making sure that land is fairly allocated between the tribes. He does this in several ways:

- For the most part, following the allocation Moses had planned for the territory east of the Jordan (Joshua 13)
- Sending three men from each tribe out to research the land (18:1–10)
- Drawing lots for other tribes to live west of the Jordan (14:1–5, 15:1–17:13, 18:11–19:48)
- Allowing some of the descendants of Joseph more land, provided they won it themselves (17:14–18)
- Making provision for female inheritance in a particular case (17:3–6)
- Giving Hebron to Caleb who had gone to spy out the land with him (14:6–15)
- Giving himself a city in the hill country of Ephraim (19:49–50)
- Assigning the Levites (the priestly tribe) cities from each of the tribal lands (21:1–42).

A further provision (chapter 20) was for six "cities of refuge", where someone who had accidentally killed a neighbour could flee to escape lynching. In such cities he could get a fair trial.

The late twentieth century saw many small communities set up, from the south side of Glasgow to Australia, by people who were searching for a shared way of life, and who wanted to offer refuge to others as in this haiku:

Place of sanctuary,
warm smile of shared acceptance,
values right way up.

## A potential conflict

Taken with what is said in Numbers, the tribes of Reuben and Gad at least have already occupied some land east of Jordan. Maybe only their fighting men have been on campaign with Joshua. Anyhow, now they go home along with half the tribe of Manasseh, and build a large altar near the river.

News of this makes the other tribes angry, and a delegation goes off to argue that this means they are in rebellion against the God of Israel, since there is to be only one holy tent for worship (22:19, echoing the call in Deuteronomy for worship at one place only). Happily, the eastern tribes are able to explain that this altar is not for worship, but to be a witness, to remind their children which God they worship. Civil war is averted.

"Just as well," said Jean. "Conflicts within the family are always the worst."

"How are things in your own family?" I asked, thinking of the visits Jean was now making to the Royal.

"I think he's glad to see me. And we talk, when he's well enough. But I'm not sure if I'm glad to see him. I know that sounds odd."

Everyone lives somewhere between that "now" and "not yet". Sometimes things seem great, with hopes fulfilled, as when Joshua confidently states (21:43–45) that they occupied the land and settled down there, all the Lord's promises fulfilled. At other times things seem bleak, as in chapter 22 when war looms on the horizon. And sometimes things seem gradually to get better, as the "much later" of 23:1 suggests.

Jean cut into our conversation. "You always try to be hopeful. All this talk about 'not yet'. But sometimes in life it's 'never'—isn't that the case?"

I had to admit it can seem like that. Thousands, millions die without seeing what they hope for. As so often, I took refuge in poetry.

### Now or Never

It was "now" for Joshua, patron of derring-do,
up-and-at-'em, *carpe diem*, Flower of Scotland
and a sporting band of optimists shot through
with pride, the flames of hope well fanned
by whisky, Bannockburn and other brew.

It was "never" finally for Moses, banned
from Canaan, given just a distant view,
forbidden entry to the promised land.
Moses never, Joshua now: but who
is judged the greater one, the guiding hand?

## Still passionate

Joshua exaggerates the progress made, in chapter 23. But when old people try to sum up their lives, and pass on lessons to the next generation, they will always simplify, to get across the main point—here, that staying faithful to Yahweh is the way to go. Was he remembering his passion as a young man to spend time in the holy tent (Exodus 33:11)?

"I notice that Joshua sees intermarriage with the Canaanites as the key thing to avoid," said Jean. "Jewish people call that 'marrying out', don't they?"

"He does, and they do. But it has nothing to do with race. If a foreigner joins forces with the God of Israel, it shouldn't be an issue, as we saw with Moses and his wives."

"But it goes further than that. The whole community has to be kept pure—we've seen that with Jews, Muslims, Catholics, Plymouth Brethren, any tight religious group."

"It can cause a lot of heartache. But it all depends how you understand that word 'pure'. I like to think of it as 'single-minded in your devotion to God', not 'outwardly belonging to our group'."

"Then it depends on how you understand 'devotion to God', doesn't it?" said Jean.

We were both painfully aware of how zeal for God has led people to do frightful things, and agreed that "love" might be a better word than "devotion". Although even love has a range of meanings, and often it is better recognised in practice than just spoken about.

Perhaps Joshua was reaching out for this in chapter 24. His address at Shechem—another central point which would keep figuring in the story of Israel up to the present day—is earthed in two ways:

1. Joshua rehearses all the things that God has done, and says in effect, "This is how God has spoken to you: God rescued you from slavery in Egypt, blessed you with a new homeland, and has given you things you did not work for."
2. Joshua says, "I and my family will serve the Lord—you do the same." He goes further and goes into dialogue with the crowd, not unlike an American Black gospel sermon.

"Why does Joshua keep telling them to get rid of their gods—I thought they were pretty thirled to the God they call 'the Lord' by this time?" queried Jean over a drink.

"I guess there are two things going on. They are doing just what believers in any age may end up doing—saying they believe in God, but being seduced by wealth, popularity, power, the usual things. The other thing was more common then than now—they bought into the idea that different gods had different territories, so although Yahweh was their God, they wanted to keep in with the Canaanite deities also, to make sure that everything was 'covered', as Rachel did back in Genesis."

The fresh covenant they entered (24:25) was a pledge of allegiance to the God of Israel alone, by all the tribes. Joshua then takes a stone, sets it up under the sacred tree, and says "it has heard all the words".

"Clever idea that," said Jean, "using a primitive notion to frighten people into obedience."

"We only think it's primitive because we are out of touch with creation. If you live close to nature, it's a natural thing to do. And of course in our poetry we have nature crying out against oil slicks and other nasty things."

### If There are Tears (Joshua 24:27)

If there are tears in things, the stones must cry
to see us throw aside our promises,
knock our faith and fellows to the ground.

If there are fears in things, the trees must try
to brace their bark against the sound of chainsaws,
pray for some miraculous turnaround.

If there are ears in things, let them hear why
the human race forgets the laws of God
to cherish, tend, stay properly earthbound.

Created things know heaven is a destiny,
not a distraction. Let them weep and wait,
while revelation nears, and look around

for signs of coming glory, then goodbye
to axes, acid rain, and all the accidents
of exploitation. Silver trumpets, sound!

"I made a promise to myself to keep on visiting Jim, even though I struggle with it. You'd think that after all these years I'd be able to forgive and forget. I don't even know if he remembers—to him it may have been a small thing, and he's been through such a lot since."

"How is Jim physically?" I asked, not quite sure where Jean wanted to take the conversation.

"Failing. I told the staff I'd visit again on Thursday if they don't ring me first."

# The end of the beginning

It was Tuesday, and we'd come to the end of Joshua 24, the bit where Joshua and Eleazar die—these two stalwarts from the time of Moses and the journey through the wilderness. Both were buried in land now belonging to their families.

### An Elegy for Eleazar

No common Israelite this one, calling Moses "uncle".
Faithful survivor, pilgrim priest, third-born of Aaron
slotted into ministry, seamless as the robes
you took from Aaron on Mount Hor, father to son.
You managed all the Levites in the holy place,
putting up that tent with all its furnishings,
the incense, lamps, anointing oil, the offerings,
knowing when and how camp should be struck.
When the red cow needed slaughter, your own finger
took its blood and made a sevenfold sprinkling
for the sins of Israelites and foreigners alike.
You knew why cedar-wood, and sprig of hyssop,
with that red cord, should catapult into the fire.

You held the key to all these mysteries,
but of your own heart, mind and soul
we have no record, save one family hint
– unlike your older brothers, your son Phinehas
knew what God required in time of crisis.
You handled gold, and tax, and holy bread;
you prayed and worked while Joshua led.

"Not everyone gets an elegy," said Jean, "but I'll make sure Jim gets a proper funeral." She had been telling me about her final visit to the Royal, on Wednesday night, when she got a phone call from ward 25. Jim's liver had finally failed, and by the time she got to the hospital, he was away.

"I was so angry with myself for not getting there earlier. But the staff were good. And they gave me a letter Jim had written some time earlier, to be handed to me after he had died."

"Do you want to tell me about it?"

"Just three words in it. 'Please forgive me.' That meant so much—and I found I could."

One part of Jean's journey had come to an end, with the book she had become part of. That closure would help her in the time that lay ahead.

I found myself thinking about those scribes in Babylon, making what sense they could of scrolls and stories they had inherited. Did they ever dream that people all round the globe would be reading them more than two thousand years later? Or were they simply immersed in their task, almost unaware that in these six books, the focus had changed from the whole universe to a single land, and from humankind to a single people?

### The Hourglass

We hardly notice how the sand grains pass
our lives, our loves so quickly through the glass;
until that tipping point, we stay cocooned
within a nest of circumstance, attuned
to family noise, the grunts and little farts
that make dull symphony, their counterparts
within the crowd just sounding much the same;
no obvious fuss, no rush to praise or blame
until the shuffle shifts its paradigm
and suddenly we all run out of time,
and fall apart. It's then God flips the scene
to let us see what all things really mean,
and how in every running grain of sand
God travels with us to the promised land.

# Notes

1   *Building Jerusalem: Elegies on Parish Churches*, ed. Kevin Gardiner (Bloomsbury, 2016).

2   See, for example, Susan Greenfield, *Mind Change* (Ebury, 2014).

3   See Iain McGilchrist, *The Master and his Emissary* (Yale University Press, 2009).

4   John Goldingay, *Joshua, Judges and Ruth for Everyone* (SPCK, 2011).

5   See Donald Wagner and Walter Davis, *Zionism and the Quest for Justice in the Holy Land* (Lutterworth Press), pp. 25–26.

6   Well-known saying of Charles Péguy (1873–1914).

7   Karl Barth, *Church Dogmatics*, IV.30 (Hendrickson Publishers Inc., 2010), p. 578.

8   James Montgomery, 1771–1854.

9   From *The Land Out There*, edited by George Bruce (Aberdeen University Press, 1991), p. 32.

10  See Adrian Curtis, *Joshua* (Sheffield Academic Press, 1994), pp. 22–25.

11  Andy Wightman, *The Poor Had No Lawyers* (Birlinn, 2013), p. 143.

# Bibliography

Archer, Jeffrey, *Kane and Abel* (Hodder & Stoughton, 1979)

Ashby, Godfrey, *Go Out and Meet God* (Eerdmans, 1998)

Barton, John and Muddiman, John (ed.), *The Pentateuch* (Oxford University Press, 2001)

Brueggemann, Walter, *The Land* (Fortress Press, 1977)

Bruce, George (ed.), *The Land Out There* (Aberdeen University Press, 1991)

Buksbazen, Victor, *The Gospel in the Feasts of Israel* (CLC, 1954)

Cairns, Ian, *Word and Presence* (Eerdmans, 1992)

Curtis, Adrian, *Joshua* (Sheffield Academic Press, 1994)

Edersheim, Alfred, *The Temple* (James Clarke, 1959)

Ellul, Jacques, *The Meaning of the City* (Eerdmans, 1970)

Francis, Gavin, *Adventures in Human Being* (Wellcome, 2015)

Goldingay, John, *Genesis for Everyone* (two volumes; SPCK, 2010)

Goldingay, John, *Exodus and Leviticus for Everyone* (SPCK, 2010)

Goldingay, John, *Numbers and Deuteronomy for Everyone* (SPCK, 2010)

Goldingay, John, *Joshua, Judges and Ruth for Everyone* (SPCK, 2011)

Gorman, Frank H jr, *Divine Presence and Community* (Eerdmans, 1997)

Harari, Yuval Noah, *Sapiens: a Brief History of Humankind* (Harper, 2014)

Howat, Irene, *Miracles from Mayhem* (Christian Focus, 2004)

Johnson, James Weldon, *God's Trombones* (Penguin Random House, 2008)

Josephus, *Antiquities of the Jews*

Kaplan, Aryeh, *Jewish Meditation* (Schocken, 1985)

Kiuchi, Nobuyoshi, *Leviticus* (IVP, 2007)

Knight, George, *Christ the Center* (Eerdmans, 1999)

Knight, George, *Theology as Narration* (Handel Press, 1977)

Knight, George, *Theology in Pictures* (Handsel Press, 1981)

Levertov, Denise, *Collected Poems* (New Directions, 2013)

Lewis, C. S., *The Last Battle: Chronicles of Narnia* (HarperCollins Children's Books, 2009)

MacNeice, Louis, *Collected Poems* (Wake Forest University Press, 2013)

McGrath, Alister, *Science and Religion: A New Introduction* (Wiley-Blackwell, 2010)

McMillen, S. I., *None of these Diseases* (Lakeland, 1973)

Mangalwadi, Vishal, *The Book that made your World* (Nelson, 2011)

Merwin, W. S., *The Shadow of Sirius* (Copper Canyon Press, 2009)

Miller, Kei, *There is an Anger that Moves* (Carcanet, 2007)

Mills, Paul and Schluter, Michael, *After Capitalism: Rethinking Economic Relationships* (Jubilee Centre, 2012)

Mlodinow, Leonard and Hawking, Stephen, *The Grand Design* (Bantam Books, 2010)

Muir, Edwin, *One Foot in Eden* (Faber & Faber, 1956)

O'Siadhail, Michael, *One Crimson Thread* (Bloodaxe, 2015)

Peterson, Eugene, *Christ Plays in Ten Thousand Places* (Hodder & Stoughton, 2005)

Provan, Iain, *Seriously Dangerous Religion* (Baylor University Press, 2014)

Roberts, Michael Symmons, *Corpus* (Cape Poetry, 2004)

Rees, Martin, *Just Six Numbers* (Orion Publishing, 1999 and 2015)

Sacks, Jonathan, *Covenant and Conversation* (Maggid, 2009)

Sacks, Jonathan, *Not in God's Name* (Hodder, 2015)

Sacks, Jonathan, *The Great Partnership* (Hodder, 2011)

Sakenfeld, Katharine, *Journeying with God* (Eerdmans, 1995)

Sedlacek, Tomas, *Economics of Good and Evil* (Oxford University Press, 2011)

Stockman, Steve, *Walk On: The Spiritual Journey of U2* (Relevant Books, 2003)

Strand, Mark, *Collected Poems* (Alfred Knopf, 2005)

Torrance, T. F., *The Mediation of Christ* (Paternoster, 1983)

Trebeck, Kerevan and Boyd, *Tackling Timorous Economics* (Luath Press, 2017)

Von Rad, Gerhard, *Deuteronomy* (SCM Press, 1966)

Wagner, Donald and Davis, Walter, *Zionism and the Quest for Justice in the Holy Land* (Lutterworth, 2014)

Wallace, Ronald S., *The Story of Joseph and the Family of Jacob* (Eerdmans, 2001)

White, Andrew, *Faith Under Fire* (Monarch, 2011)

Wightman, Andy, *The Poor Had No Lawyers* (Birlinn, 2013)

Wilson, A. N., *The Book of the People* (Atlantic Books, 2015)

Wright, Tom, *Surprised by Scripture* (SPCK, 2014)

Zagajewski, Adam, *Eternal Enemies*, tr. from Polish by Clare Cavanagh (Farrar, Straus and Giroux, 2008)

# Index of Names and Places

# Index of Books and Films, Poems and Paintings

*With the author's poems in italics*

# Index of Topics

# Index of Scripture References